A Gracious Space: Winter Edition

Brave Writer LLC 7723 Tylers Place Blvd. #165
West Chester, OH 45069

Website: www.bravewriter.com

Brave Writer 2015

Author: Julie Bogart
Cover Photography: Tammy Wahl
Typesetting: Sara McAllister

First published in 2015

ISBN-10: 099051336X
ISBN-13: 978-0-9905133-6-0

Contents

Brave Writer

Brave Writer

Winter: A Gracious Space

Preface

A Gracious Space is a collection of thoughts and reflections on home education drawn from personal experience and the lives of thousands of Brave Writer families. The winter collection continues the tradition of fall—and is intended to sustain you through the colder, indoor months. The desire to "re-up" your commitment after the holidays is powerful. This volume supports that aspiration and is meant to help you follow through on your best intentions for your family and homeschool.

All of us seek support—whether in the form of in-person cooperatives or online communities. This series of daily readings is drawn from the daily posts I've shared on the Brave Writer Facebook page and blog. Apparently they struck a nerve: many of the entries generated hundreds of likes, shares, and comments. We are releasing one volume of these mini-essays per season to support you in your homeschooling vision and practice.

This second volume has 50 entries for winter. Pair one per day with a cup of tea or coffee, and remind yourself of your values and your value. Each entry is accompanied by a comment from a parent like you or notable person and a daily sustaining thought. These thoughts make wonderful source material for your own copywork, which you could do right alongside your children and a lovely lit candle. Try it. You may find that you are more inclined to enjoy the quiet moments of the day if you write with your children and calm yourself with soothing supportive thoughts that relate to this demanding lifestyle.

Remember to be kind not only to your children, but to yourself. You're learning how to be a home educator even as you educate your children. No two years are alike, and each season of a single year will have its own character. The winter is a time when unit studies, reading aloud, and handcrafts are popular. Take advantage of your fireplace (if you have one). One family I know used to roast marshmallows in the fireplace during read aloud time! The point is that you can enhance the experience of home education when the doors are closed to the cold outside world by attending to the particular nature of winter—a time to pull in and dive deep, to play board games and read books.

The topics included in this volume cover a range of principles and practices that apply to any homeschooling family. Feel free to read them a day at a time, or in a rush all at once. You might also find these readings useful at homeschool support group meetings. Read an entry as your meeting begins and use it as a perspective for discussion or consolation.

It gives me great joy to watch parents free themselves of the external pressure to perform according to someone else's standards or vision for their homeschool. As you develop your own homeschool lifestyle, remember that it will look like you—your particular family. If you need more support on the journey, feel free to check out the

Brave Writer

homeschool coaching and mentoring program I offer at: http://coachjuliebogart.com/. The Homeschool Alliance is designed to give you additional support and help you explore your vision to tailor-make your homeschool.

Enjoy this volume!

Keep going.

Day 1

Throw it at the Wall. See What Sticks!

Let me introduce you to "play." That is, I'd like you to play with your homeschooling tools. Rather than focusing so much on "getting it right" and "scheduling enough time" and "completing the objectives," what if you saw your manuals, your books, the pastels for artwork, the piano, your yardsticks and calculators, computers and binoculars, writing prompts, dissection kits, vocabulary cards, and field guides as toys in a big box waiting to be opened and discovered?

What if you skipped chapters and went straight for the single most interesting concept in the entire book (and it turned out to come nearly at the end, rather than at the beginning)? What would happen if you tried to build the catapult before you had learned how to hammer nails? Wouldn't you find yourself suddenly far more interested in nail-hammering with this fascinating project in front of you that can't continue until you've got the basics mastered for balancing the little nail between your fingers and smashing it with a swing of the hammer? Sometimes the end leads us to the beginning, and that leads us to enthusiasm!

What if when you read a chapter about revision in writing, you scan for the one key idea that stimulates brand new thoughts, and skip all the insipid ones about tightening

 Brave Writer

your sentences or embellishing skimpy paragraphs with additional detail? What if you simply went for the best, brightest idea, such as: hiding a secret, or foreshadowing a future event within the budding story?

If this grabs hold of your attention, go for it!

Why not?

Why not play with the toys of your curriculum? If you try a little, you might find you develop a taste for it all. These tools are under your command. You get to decide how to use them. It's perfectly fine to throw your attempts at a wall and see what sticks, rather like testing spaghetti noodles for their "doneness."

The most difficult part of being a home educator is that you feel you are flying blindly. As a result, you put far too much trust into the textbooks and materials, as though they hold the keys to educating your young. But they don't. They offer you a possible pathway to mastery—that is it!

As the one in charge, you can determine which pieces actually accomplish that goal!

Not only that—please enjoy the educational process.

If you open The Writer's Jungle, for instance, and you find yourself curious about "dumb writing assignments," why wouldn't you skip directly to that chapter and read it!? It might scratch your itch.

It's okay if your child hates the Topic Funnel or resists the study of "literary elements" for today. That's just today. Find some other tidbit worth enjoying and exploring. You may circle back to the items that were resisted and have more success once a child "buys in" through joy in another aspect of the program (whatever program - not just mine).

I literally have no stake in anyone approving every teaching I offer. I have a huge stake in your happiness at home with your children. I would imagine you do too, or you wouldn't even attempt this slightly demented program of educating your children of multiple grade levels all day every day without a break from your charges.

You can trace the birds in the field guide without ever looking at a real bird, if that is what suits you. You can choose to never read poetry at teatime and instead only read geography terms or watch movies.

Your homeschool is under your control. But even more than that, it is meant to be wonderful. Play with the materials. See what happens when you allow your imagination to fuse with the orderly structure of the texts.

You may find, for instance, that jumping rope while skip counting is more fun than doing it at a table.

You may find that emailing the child's father at work the five amazing facts about his favorite football team is more engaging for your young student than writing a mini report.

Try a little. Test it. See how it feels. Skip what disinterests you. Trust the process, not the product. Trust yourself, not the invisible educator not present in the room.

Brave Writer

My goodness! You are all adults. You know what you know and you know how to find out what you don't know and you won't cover it all anyway, and what you do together with your children is going to be enough because you can never do it all.

Anything you miss? I promise, they will meet it again in college or they will never need it again (or they can AskJeeves).

Let loose a little. January is a good time for that.

Quote of the day

I'm just going to apply it to my whole life!

Kim Suzanne Stewart

Sustaining thought

Sometimes the end leads us to the beginning, and that leads us to enthusiasm!

Day 2

Take Pictures of the Daily Stuff!

Our family put together a slide show for Liam (fourth child, before he left for his summer job as an IT guy at camp, and then on to college). I was struck the most by the photos of our ordinary life. Sure, pictures are always a part of vacations and births, holidays and when the relatives come. But the photos I love the most? Two kids lying on their backs, heads touching, on the trampoline; a cup of hot cocoa the size of a small planet sitting in front of a six-year-old's toothless smile; the laptop open with four kids watching the same screen; Kitchen Aid mixing the bread dough for bread bears; snuggling toddlers in the same bed; each kid reading a favorite book . . .

I have so many photos of our homeschool years—priceless now that I can never take them again.

The social media craze gives you occasion to share these daily moments in ways I never imagined when my kids were young. I know most of you are used to taking pictures constantly.

You don't need to miss the event in order to take pictures (I get that that is not useful! Sometimes just being there is enough). But pictures of tying shoes and making grilled cheese sandwiches may be some of your better shots and you can sneak these in when no one is thinking about posing for the camera.

 Brave Writer

I spent one year taking a picture a day (at least one) and posting it to my blog. That did more to teach me about photography and to pay attention to the small, unnoticed moments than any other photography advice. I still use that year's worth of photos more than any other!

You might try it.

Bottom line: it all goes quickly. I'm really glad I got to spend all those hours admiring my children. I'm equally glad I took pictures of them.

Quote of the day

A good snapshot stops a moment from running away.

Eudora Welty

Sustaining thought

Capture the small everyday stuff on film—the goings-on that you might otherwise miss and then forget later. You'll never regret it.

Day 3

Are Speech and Writing Related?

A debate exists about writing: Is it related to speech? If so, how much? If not, why not?

One camp says that learning to write is akin to learning to speak a foreign language. Writing is as foreign to native speakers of any language as Amharic is to you or me (unless you are Ethiopian!). That's why children struggle to become fluent writers, so the thinking goes. Children are naturally wired for speech and are frustrated trying to translate those words into language suitable for writing (the style of it, the vocabulary of it, the spelling of it, the punctuating of it, the organizing of it, the handwriting or typing of it). Even my guru, Peter Elbow, says that some people feel as if they are translating speech into something else when they write. Have you ever experienced the "Hmmm, how shall I say this?" thought as you sit down to actually write the thought you are having?

That's what this camp is getting at. There's a weird translation process between speech and writing. Because so many of us have experienced that moment, there's a sense in which it must be true: writing must be so different from speech, we are prone to writer's block as a result.

There is a bit of truth in this perspective. The brain is not

 Brave Writer

wired for writing, like it is for speech. Writing is a learned activity. Speech, however, is hardwired into all human beings.

The other camp sees writing as related to speech. Dr. Peter Elbow, again, recently published an entire book (*Vernacular Eloquence*) that attempts to make this case to a resistant academy. Writing is the extension of speech, he argues. If we can understand speech first, and then see how it informs and creates writing, we will wave a wand of release over thousands of frozen would-be writers. The mechanics are only one aspect of writing—writing actually sits inside each of us as native speakers already.

What is fascinating is that in the world of homeschooling programs, both views rely on copywork, dictation, and two varieties of narration (oral and written) to help students gain fluency in "writing." But their starting points of view are polar opposites.

What I've noticed in my work with thousands of families is that children are more inclined to put in the effort of learning the skills associated with writing when they can see that it relates to a skill they have already mastered: The English language.

When we talk about putting their thoughts into written words, we are asking them to identify thoughts! In Brave Writer, I suggest you "catch your child in the act of thinking." Help your child discover that he or she is having thoughts worthy of record: write them down when they least expect it, when you hear those thoughts tumbling out of their mouths!

Every single day your children are not only thinking thoughts, but using those thoughts to generate oral language. That language can easily become written language when they have a transcriptionist (you!).

Once the connection is made ("What's inside my head and comes out of my mouth can also be what shows up on paper and is read to others"), teaching the mechanics of writing becomes much more interesting to children. They get it—writing is about their mind lives and they love sharing those thoughts with others.

Are there style differences between writing and speaking? Of course! Are there pesky rules of grammar and syntax that we follow when writing but often break when speaking? Naturally.

But if we start by seeing writing as foreign (a foreign language), if we begin with the assumption that says that writing is "hard work" and that the "discipline" of writing requires rote work with someone else's words first, if we suggest that what is inside your child will not be suited to the page until some kind of mastery is achieved in handwriting or spelling, we literally alienate the fluent native speaker from writing—from believing in his or her writing voice before it has uttered a written peep!

That alienation, time and again, manifests as writer's block or not caring. The spark of individuality that is your child is lost in all this "hard work of precision and accuracy." Accuracy matters, but it is not more important than originality of thought. Accuracy can be added; originality can be lost.

 Brave Writer

What studies are showing to be true is that children are far more likely to take writing risks when they believe that their content is valuable, and when they trust their thought lives to be adequate to self-expression. They are more likely to work on their mechanics if they experience the mechanics as supporting their original thoughts, rather than having to show perfect mechanics before they are permitted to have original thoughts.

If we value our children's thought lives, help them to express themselves in Big Juicy Conversations, if we transcribe some of their ideas and read them back later to our children, if we ask for expansion of thoughts and show curiosity, if we model language choices that are more likely to be associated with written language models, our children will absolutely discover writing in much the same way they found speech!

They will risk, test, try, show off, back away, make huge silly errors, make leaps of logic, express vocabulary beyond their years, will imitate and create, startle and master, and sometimes mess with you acting like they don't have a thing to say. But they will grow! This is what growth looks like.

The approach we use in Brave Writer does not see writing as a foreign or antagonistic process that requires painful hard work. Rather, we see writing as the opportunity to take speech further—to enhance, expand, and nourish speech (oral language, inner thought), and then to preserve and share it with interested audiences.

Kids respond well to this vision of writing. They love to read, to be read to, to talk and converse. Writing, particularly in today's dialogical world of the Internet, is another conversational tool. We can learn how to wield writing for a variety of audiences, but why not start with the one closest to home? Why not let them write for themselves? Then for you, and then for their friends, and finally for "academic purposes." This is the progression that works.

I hope you feel reassured. You are not teaching Hindi to your kids, with a whole new language structure and vocabulary. Writing in one's native tongue is built from the English already spoken and understood. Writing is simply gaining mechanical skills to transcribe one's own fluent thoughts, and learning how to develop these thoughts into the flow of written language.

Brave Writer has created oodles of tools and tactics to help kids "get it." We've got more in the pipeline.

You can help your kids learn to write well. Start from the idea that your children are writers already, learning mechanical skills, in search of a supportive editor/reader: you.

You can do it!

And so can they!

 Brave Writer

Quote of the day

Thank you for this. It sums up what I've been doing with my child for the past three years! When I pulled him out of school due to LD, I quickly realized the relationship of writing to speech. We did lots of talking that first year....telling and re-telling of stories. Things are mug better now but we still talk it out before each and every writing assignment....well worth the extra few minutes of my time:)

Karen Anne

Sustaining thought

You foster natural growth in writing in a similar way to how you helped your child become a fluent speaker of English: through admiration, modeling, enthusiasm and freedom to take risks.

Day 4

Beware of "Open and Go"

The "resort on a beach" of all curricula is the "Open and Go" variety. You receive the UPS box in the mail, crack the spine of the new workbook or text, and immediately know what to do, right now, with your kids, without any preparation, reading of instructions, or adoption of a particular philosophy.

This magical product teaches the tough subject you have avoided without taxing you, plus your kids like it! What a bargain!

So do these products work for writing? More specifically, does Brave Writer have a product like this? Please, Mother may I?

Writing is unlike content-oriented subject matter. You aren't exposing your children to a list of facts or details and asking them to memorize or consume them. Writing isn't a set of formulae to be introduced and practiced. Writing isn't the coordination of handwriting, punctuation, spelling, and grammar that can be learned in workbook formats. Writing is more than any of these, even if at times it embodies all of them.

Writing—original writing—is created from thoughts. Thoughts are personal to the writer. Thoughts come first.

 Brave Writer

Everything else is window dressing.

Just as speech required a context for risk and communication with an active partner, so, too, writing requires a witness and compassionate reader. Writing thrives when it becomes a dialogue between the author and his or her audience—particularly the audience of an invested parent.

Scripting that dialogue is not possible. A set of workbook pages doesn't get at the mind life of the child. Writing forms can't instruct the process of self-inquiry (which is the genesis of all good writing). Handing our children a set of instructions to be read alone, and a book with lines on the page to fill in, doesn't help them imagine themselves as writers. Rather they are being taught that writing is external to self, done for that page, according to someone else's ideas of what should go there.

Literally— 'open and go' workbook writing programs ask children to think of writing as a task done according to someone else's prescription of what goes "over there" away from self. Children are taught to think that the thoughts for writing exist inside someone else's vision, and their job is to hunt them down (pluck them from the thin air) and hope they've collected enough of them in one place to get a "good grade."

This is not writing. This is puzzle solving—holding the directions in the mind, while wrestling language into the imagined form the assignment creator may have intended.

Yet this "assignment writing in a workbook" is the holy grail of writing instruction! Can't parents hand a book to their children and ask them to follow the clear instructions? Won't writing grow with practice? What about all those writing assignments in high school and college? Kids don't get to pick their topics or formats then, do they? Why not practice now?

Parents, typically, don't have good memories of writing instruction from their childhoods, and many are not self-confident writers today. Yet many programs expect parents to instruct children in writing using similar methods that didn't work all that well for them. These programs lead to similar results—mediocre, unconfident writing. That's not to say that some kids don't find their way to brilliance and enthusiasm! Writers (kids who love writing) find their way regardless of method, half the time.

Helpful writing instruction requires a philosophy that is a paradigm shift away from how you, the parent, likely learned to write. The shift is in focus—away from form and accuracy as primary, and toward risk and expression as essential. Original writing is about how the mind generates thought—instruction is about how you foster an environment for creative thinking and use of language to grow. It's about recognizing that writing is more than words on a page, but is, rather, the valuing of the writer's own perspective of the world—a writer's personal experiences and values, curiosities, mastery of facts, passionate reads, hopes and aspirations, confusions and frustrations, challenges and arguments, connection to others, and reporting of information.

This is writing. All writing is this—this distillation of an

Brave Writer

individual's mind life/thought world. Clarity and accuracy matter, but so do inspiration, imagination, critical thinking, and flexible, expanded vocabulary. Form helps to manage these aspects of the topic for writing, but forms can also stifle original thought. Knowing how to write means knowing how to manage the forms, rather than be managed by them.

All this to say: "open and go" deprives writing of its essential context—space and room to explore. Can you imagine asking for an "open and go" parenting manual? "Open and go" driver's training? "Open and go" sexuality and reproduction workbook?

When we are dealing with danger, complexity, values, intimate relationships, connection, or thought lives, we do our children a disservice to think we can teach them by opting out of the hard work of engaging with them. True partnership and dialogue go more slowly, but so much more richly.

Brave Writer has materials and classes that support the relationship of new writer to parent-coach. We even give you specific words to say, and processes and practices to try together. These are tools that can be used again and again as your young writers learn to internalize the self-inquiry style of writing generation. We give you projects to test together—with week-by-week instructions of what to do. But in each case, all the way until high school, your presence—your appreciation for and understanding of the process, your conversation and modeling—is essential.

Make time and space for writing in your family. It can look like teatime and poetry on some days. It can look like family movie night or read-aloud time or freewriting or riddle creating or limerick reciting. It may be the hard work of jotting down an endless story or the wise support you offer a teen trying to start a blog about recycling. Writing instruction might include the hard work of grammar study or learning to edit for spelling errors. But it isn't essentially that. It is the discovery of what one has to say that is worth preserving and presenting in a cogent manner.

Writing is unlike any other subject in homeschool. In fact, it's not a subject. Writing is about writers. Writers need readers. You are the reader—the partner, coach, and ally your child deserves, as you help your writers discover their voices, their vocabularies, and their powers of refining their messages in the written word.

No "open and go" workbook can show you how to do that. You need to live it alongside your kids, once you've adopted the principles into your heart. It's a privilege to be that person in your child's life. Don't delegate it to a workbook! Yes, it takes time. So do all the things you care most about.

Surprisingly, teaching writing this way is so pleasurable it doesn't feel like work any more. It feels like relationship. A good, rich one. The kind you want with your kids—the kind that lets you into their minds and hearts.

So worth it.

Quote of the day

Boy did I need to hear this. As a mom with three kids and two of which have special needs, we spend much of our time on the go and I was thinking, we need the perfect workbook, this article calmed me. Thank you!

Jen Fischer Midkiff

Sustaining thought

What a privilege it is to be the one that encourages your children to open their minds and hearts in writing and then to share it.

Day 5

Don't Overthink

You want to do a good job of parenting?

Think less about how to shape your kids into world changers and more about how to bring a wide world to your family to shape them.

Think less about turning your kids into responsible mini adults and more about how to ensure they have a childhood.

Think more about how much energy your children invest in what they love and less about what they fail to do.

Think more about each child's natural aptitudes and less about each child's deficiencies.

Think less about the future and more about today—this moment.

Think less about expert advice and more about your hunches.

Think more of your children than the Famous People who Write about Them.

Think less about disciplinary tactics and more about "live and let live."

Think less of yourself (your power to impact who your

 Brave Writer

children become) and more about the innate power of genetics, culture, language, and nationality.

Allow yourself to be in awe; disallow anxiety.

Think more about what you can control (your own character and maturity) and less about what you can't (your children's).

Think more of your child's responsibility to grow up to be who he or she is, and less of your ability to make some imagined outcome happen.

Think only of your responsibility to provide possibilities and opportunities, and less of your obligation to guarantee outcomes (to anyone—the state, your spouse, your extended family, yourself).

Let yourself off the hook—you are limited. Celebrate your limits.

Let your kids off the hook—they are limited. Enjoy their limits.

Think about all the signs of maturity, character, intelligence, and heart you do see; think less about the recklessness, slip-shod work ethic, bickering, and lack of academic progress that reminds you they are still minors.

Think more of yourself than you usually do. You are enough, you have the right kids, you know what it means to love and educate them. You do it every day.

Think less of the revered friends and experts. They are not

you. They do what they do. They don't have your kids. They can't parent for you. They shouldn't live in your head.

Think more about developing thinkers (people who engage ideas) and less about getting your kids through an education (people who pass classes).

Think more of home education when you are at home, defending it to yourself, and defend it less to other people.

You do know what you're doing. The tweaks and changes you make are validations of your vision, not invalidations of past choices. You are growing alongside your children, becoming an educator as you go.

Think more of your journey as a homeschooler, and less about what your kids are learning.

If you value your growth, you'll learn to value your kids' growth.

If you love what you are learning about education and learning, your kids will find some version of that lifestyle for themselves. It's contagious.

If you are undistracted by the flaws in your system, personality, finances, and home life and think more about how to become intimate with a subject area that fascinates you, your entire life (including homeschool and children) will flourish.

Don't overthink this one. Stay the course, learn, grow, share, *trust*.

 Brave Writer

You are less important in the total scheme of things than you realize, and you are far more valuable in the moment-to-moment day-by-day than you appreciate.

Both are true.

Don't overthink it.

Quote of the day

Stop spying on me. Lol. Wow—so timely.

Hall Family

Sustaining thought

Think less. Live more!

Day 6

Good Thinkers or Good Students?

In your efforts to create a context for learning, don't be seduced by the idea of raising "good students." Good students learn the material, pass the courses, obey the rules, complete the assigned pages, move ahead through pre-determined increments of "learning acquisition," and fulfill your objectives.

"Good thinkers," on the other hand, can be a pain in the home educator's behind! They will challenge the reasonableness of a particular course of study, will camp on one idea until they've exhausted it (and you!), will ask questions (sometimes endless questions with greater and greater detail required to answer them), show persistence in one particular line of inquiry while not giving a rip about any other (especially if the other topics feel unrelated to the current area of fascination), and they appear argumentative.

Good students receive information so they may get credit for the course of study.

Good thinkers consume information so they generate understanding.

Good students study information to pass a test.

Good thinkers put their findings to the test.

 Brave Writer

Good students forget the information once the subject is "completed" and credit is earned.

Good thinkers retain what they learned because they know they will need it in their real lives.

Good students hope to reduce the complexity of a topic by organizing it into the essential bullet points.

Good thinkers poke at the topic until they find the inconsistency or problem within it, creating a morass of complexity.

Good students read the assignments.

Good thinkers read widely.

Good students don't argue with experts.

Good thinkers argue with anyone.

Good students master a particular set of terms to use in papers.

Good thinkers develop a rich vocabulary that becomes an organic feature of that student's language use.

Good students quote the insights of others in their papers.

Good thinkers generate insight.

Good students remember some of what they studied.

Good thinkers remember what they learned.

Good students learn each subject area as though unrelated to the next.

Good thinkers correlate one set of ideas with another set from some other course of study, creating an inter-relatedness of all their areas of interest.

Good students throw away their notes and lessons once they've completed the course.

Good thinkers save their work because they might need it again.

Of course there are good thinkers in public schools and good students at home, and vice versa.

But the opportunity to be a "good thinker" is much more easily achieved at home! Do your best to promote "good thinking." It takes being willing to let go of your approval of "good student" behaviors so that you will notice and affirm "good thinker" ones instead.

Good luck!

Quote of the day

This is so affirming. Especially when our good thinkers don't look much like good students.

Jennifer Breseman

Sustaining thought

Good thinking parents nurture good thinking children.

Day 7

Keep the Focus Pure

The competing demands on your time will eventually eat into your homeschool. You will ping-pong between getting your kids out of the house into the big world so that they have experiences, meet other children, learn from passionate adults, and become skilled athletes, musicians, dancers, or pet rescuers, to utter seclusion where you shut the doors against that big world, and stay happily home steadily making progress in the subject areas of "school"—until you get tired of the routine and burst back onto the world's stage.

This back-and-forth is common among homeschoolers, and works great for many of them. For some families, it's a seasonal thing. In my family, for instance, we kept the sanest "stay-at-home" schedule in winter quarter while indulging a much more energetic out-of-home schedule in fall and spring (coinciding with soccer and lacrosse practices).

Even so, you can feel like too little butter spread over so much bread, trying to keep up with the competing beliefs you have about a healthy, happy homeschool and childhood.

Opt out of that maze of confusion and adopt a different rubric. Fix your gaze on your individual children, and your children as a group. They are the focus. They are the rubric.

Ask yourself these questions:

1. Who is left out?

2. What needs have I catered to and which ones have I overlooked?

3. What can I cut? Or, conversely, what can I add?

4. Which child is the most vocal about his or her needs? Which one holds them in?

5. Why am I [adding in/taking out] this activity? Am I trying to please someone else?

6. If I could have a week the way I want it, would it look like the week I'm currently having? What one thing can I do to make it look more like what I wish it were?

7. Am I doing any of my activities out of guilt? Which ones?

8. Are there any activities that my child can do without me?

9. Are we having fun yet?

Your kids need your attention—not your philosophy or your community or your fears and worries. During 15+ years of homeschooling, you will undulate between seasons of intense community involvement and quiet spans of time in at-home peacefulness. Balance isn't always achieved week to week. Sometimes it is achieved over an entire childhood. That's okay!

I remember that with five children, we made a rule that only two kids could play sports at any one time. That was our only route to sanity with all the driving involved.

Think about how your family functions best in this season and do that. You'll know when that season needs to change by how your children are behaving, performing, and holding up. You'll know it by how you are feeling, too. At that moment, don't beat yourself up! Simply recognize it's time for a shift in the routine. Follow through and enjoy that season as long as it lasts.

Keep your focus pure.

Quote of the day

Love this. Another item I put on the checklist is "have a mission statement." Sounds kinda cheesy, but having your goals for your children (and their own goals) written out is a really nice way to prioritize activities. Sort of a touchstone for their education.

Lori Bleau

Sustaining thought

When it's time for a shift in your homeschooling routine, you'll know because you're keeping your focus pure.

Day 8

No One Likes to be Criticized

No one.

You don't. You don't want someone to examine what you do in your homeschool and tell you that you've got it wrong.

I don't. I don't like being examined and found wanting.

Writers don't. They risk putting themselves out there. Even if what they risk appears paltry and disconnected from what they care about, they still recoil from editorial feedback.

Yet we all want to grow and become better versions of ourselves. Don't we? In our most honest moments?

It takes some toughness to be open to criticism. There's a reason for this. Criticism exposes mistakes. The experience of being mistaken is painful. You feel exposed—there it is, your failure, out there for all to see.

No one likes that feeling. Worse, if you are seeking support and feedback, getting criticism in return can feel like a betrayal of trust. You shared your struggle using the words available to you, and this other person picked them apart or misheard your intention or cared only about her superior understanding and appeared to take pleasure in her reconstruction of the "right way."

 Brave Writer

There's a way to deliver feedback that doesn't leave the recipient undone, devastated, hurt, and embarrassed. It's the chief feature of our writing instruction, and is at the heart of how I operate in my family and business.

I follow these principles because they ensure emotional safety, while allowing dialogue for growth.

1. Value the person.

Your child, your spouse, your best friend, the member of your email list or discussion board, needs to know that you value him or her first. The human being taking the risk to share "self" with you must feel that she is valuable, essentially worthy of care and consideration. That comes from the tedious, time-consuming task of using words, facial expressions, and internal postures that remind you that in fact, this person is worthy of my time/energy/care. Most people want to be good people, or regarded as such, which is a sound enough basis from which to begin.

Your kids want to be good kids, want to please you, want to do what they are supposed to do to become full-fledged adults. They want your guidance, too. Most spouses want to be loved and to give love back. Most best friends want to be trusted allies. Most participants on most lists and boards want to be heard and helped.

Yes, there are exceptions, but let's start with the rule: Most human beings seek connection, and want a mirror that tells them: "I see you. You matter."

2. Failure is painful.

The failure to live up to one's own vision of success (successful living—homeschooling, marriage, career, writing a paragraph, being a teammate, running a household, parenting, managing finances, exercise and diet, calculating percentages in an online game) is painful. All by itself. This must be appreciated before offering a critique. Even the cavalier, half-hearted effort is often a cover for not wanting to risk full-commitment to avoid giving a best effort and failing still. Better to only "half-try" and then when criticized you can tell yourself, "I wasn't really trying." This half-effort protects the ego because what if you gave a full effort and still failed? That would mean you were fundamentally flawed, unable to grow/succeed. "What more can be given than a 'full effort,'?" goes the unconscious reasoning.

So before feedback, it's important to have full appreciation for the pain of failure. Your comments are about to land someone in that pain (particularly if delivered with judgment, anger, or exasperation).

3. Frame your feedback in the positive by giving information, not criticism.

"Looks to me like you wanted the reader to pause here. We use a comma for that."

Is much better than:

"You left out a comma."

© Julie (Bogart) Sweeney | bravewriter.com   Brave Writer

Or as one of our instructors says, she likes to use "Remember to..." rather than "Don't forget to..." Even a simple switch to a positive is better received than a negative.

The premise is that everyone is trying their best. Even when they aren't, they can be inspired to try their best when we find glimpses of effort behind the half-try.

"I'm so glad you answered the question. I look forward to reading more answers from you this week."

Much better than:

"You aren't giving me enough material to read so I can comment. I expect more later this week."

I've noticed that homeschool discussion board conversations devolve when the original poster asks a question, not using the evolved vocabulary of the group, and is then challenged for her errant thinking. This experience leads to online flailing: the need to reframe, restate, explain away. The original poster will then try to give some sense of her inner process to justify her poorly worded question, which is batted away by the experts.

Some people are strong enough for that kind of aggressive help. But many are not. Most children are not.

It helps to receive the intention of the person first, to value the desire to connect, or to ask for help, or to share first efforts in work. It helps to remember that failing is painful, and that having a failure pointed out is exposing and embarrassing. What works at that point is supportive, positive feedback that takes into account the whole person, not just their weakness or failure to perform at the desired level.

You get there through the self-discipline of thinking in a new way. Take time to find it. Your child isn't lazy. Your child simply didn't do the work. Ask yourself why. Think about how you might support a change in atmosphere around the topic, or help your child to see the benefits of effort, even small, short bursts of concentration. Start there rather than berating a person's character.

Your child isn't addicted to video games. He loves playing them. He gets things from them that make him happy. What is he getting? What can you learn about video games to understand why he is so absorbed? What else can you offer him in his life that is also compelling, and could be of interest to him?

Or conversely, is it possible that something "not good" is happening in his world and video games are giving him a way of escape? Can you find out?

Conversations that are non judgmental, curiosity-seeking, supportive explorations will lead to receptivity more than labels and reactionary anger.

Sometimes we all lose our cool and say mean things or jump to conclusions. Sometimes we're right—the other person is being mean-spirited or recalcitrant and is not receptive to input from us. Sometimes we are in abusive relationships! No amount of supportive dialogue will yield good results.

 Brave Writer

But on the whole, a practice of this kind will bring about trust, support, and growth. That's how we grow brave writers, in fact. And it works beautifully.

Quote of the day

Thank you for this.

Alicia Bennett

Sustaining thought

Thinking in a new and positive way brings new and positive results.

Day 9

Peace and Progress

Peace: you all get along with each other, the house is humming with happy energy, projects and play are in full flow, there's enough food in the cabinets, a satisfying mess reassures you that your kids are engaged, not bored and dissatisfied.

Progress: today is a little better than yesterday, you got a little further in the plan, someone understood what was not understood yesterday, someone else applied a new skill, you kept calm when you wanted to yell, one child helped another child when asked.

Peace: you trust your instincts, you listen to the feeling messages your children express and are open to them, you put connection ahead of expectation, you turn away from standards imposed on you, you pat yourself on the back when you accomplish a single goal, you offered help rather than scolding.

Progress: you measure new aspects of education—concentration, effort put forth, attempts, risks, asking for help, trying again after failing, initiative, creativity, originality, problem-solving, attention to detail, making connections between subject areas.

Peace: you remember that you love who your children are today more than your vision of who you hope they will become.

 Brave Writer

Progress: you note and celebrate the achievements your children value in themselves—the new soccer skill, the ability to hiccup 60 times in a row, the block tower, the house of cards, beating a sibling in Yu-Gi-Oh! cards, sliding down the stairs headfirst like an Olympic luge competitor.

We want peace and progress. Let those be the measurements. How might you foster peace and facilitate progress in your homeschool? How might you measure in a way that serves you and your children?

Quote of the day

Peace begins with a smile.

Mother Teresa

Sustaining thought

Put connection ahead of expectation.

Day 10

Slow Down

Slow down, you move too fast
You got to make the morning last
—Paul Simon

To feel groovy, you have to let yourself move slowly, savor, find a rhythm and stick to it, meander.

Home education is a trip on side streets.

It's the wasted time of sleeping in and running late and questions such as, "Where is my other shoe?"

It's the long straggly gaggle of children, strollers, and backpacks making their way across a crowded, dangerous parking lot to a museum. Inside, an hour spent looking at three paintings is plenty. It leads to sidetracked conversations about "unrelated" subjects and what is retained is hidden from view for years (maybe a decade). Then the whole kit and caboodle reverses course to saunter and dawdle back to the car where the buckling, clicking, and tucking in take longer because everyone is tired and hungry.

Home education means charging forward with new materials and slogging slowly through old, comfortable ones.

When lightning strikes (She's reading! He finished his story! She mastered the 7's! He learned all the capitals!), celebration takes time and words, and uses up treats in the toy box or refrigerator. Happiness has room to be felt and known. Personal pride is admired. Nothing more is accomplished in the basking glow of success.

Homeschool means that when a child begs to be read the next chapter, we do even if it means staying up a little later—who can stop when everyone (including Mom or Dad) is so eager to know what happens next?

Math is ditched when *Nova* is airing an episode about the migration habits of your favorite birds. All manner of family members hunker down under blankets to let the visual feast of scenes unspool at their deliberate unhurried pace.

Making muffins for teatime lasts an eternity of measuring the ingredients, struggling to stir the messy mix, and unevenly filling the cups, only to bake them and wait, wait, wait for the wonderfully yummy end results.

No one wants to stop reading poetry...ever. So some days you don't stop, and it's wonderfully okay.

When the sun comes out after its long absence, kicking a soccer ball in the backyard is on task and feels right. No one misses the phonics workbook that day yet everyone knows it's not gone forever. Just for today—this one glorious long day of nothing but sunshine.

Take time today—to be, float, notice, hang, enjoy, savor.

Homeschooling is a magnificent waste of time—it refuses to be boxed into systems, schedules, and requirements.

It is the long, lazy, loving look at learning through the eyes of children.

It takes time—time you don't have, time you aren't used to spending in all your adult hurry. Give in. Let go.

Feel groovy.

Quote of the day

We spent today at a science center and I was almost about to scold myself for not "doing school" today. Thanks.

Liz Davis

Sustaining thought

Home education is a trip on side streets.

Brave Writer

Day 11

A Lot Depends on You

This is both good news and bad news. The good news is that you set the tone, make the choices, create the energy, and foster an environment of peace and learning.

The bad news is that it is up to you to set the tone, make the choices, create the energy, and foster an environment of peace and learning.

Sometimes we all wish we had a little less power and responsibility, right? Sometimes it's a lot to carry, and we don't realize it until our shoulders are slumped and we miss scheduled appointments or forget important deadlines.

If this is you—if the work you do to ensure peace and well-being at home is sapping your vibrancy and optimism—I want to be a voice today that says: "I see that. I appreciate you."

- Thanks for getting up in the middle of the night— again—with the baby and bed-wetter.

- Thank you for holding back your tired, angry voice.

- Thank you for hunkering down with a curriculum you don't like but can't afford to replace right now.

- Thank you for making magic with vegetables and healthy snacks for reluctant-to-try-anything-new kids.

- Thank you for overlooking the insensitive jab from your trusted partner because s/he is stressed and being a blockhead.

- Thank you for examining your motives.

- Thanks for exercising and/or eating right and/or taking your meds and/or trying hard to be healthy when it's easier to give up.

- Thanks for excusing childishness.

- Thank you for celebrating childishness.

- Thank you for being childlike with your children!

- Thank you for being the chief source of comfort to your teen who sometimes doesn't even like you.

- Thanks for calling that friend, or your mother, or the sibling that wears you out because they needed you today.

- Thank you for keeping house as best you can, in spite of the never-ending assault on your house by all the people who love you but love your house less.

- Thank you for washing an unending parade of dishes, for laundering every last pair of socks, for cleaning behind the couches once a year, for hanging pretty things to look at on the walls.

- Thank you for research, and appointments scheduled, and payments made on time, and performances attended with camera and heart in hand.

- Thank you for not falling apart.

- Thank you for holding it together long after you thought you couldn't.

The work you do is invisible to many but well known to all of us who lead the same life you do. Well done!

Life morphs and changes; demands emerge and fade. Pay attention to your life; make choices that ensure the peace and well-being of your loved ones.

That responsibility does fall to you, and we can be grateful that it does. With power comes responsibility. Keep using it wisely.

As I like to say: "Keep going."

Quote of the day

"To foster an environment of peace and learning." Perfect way to sum up the way the homeschool is a lifestyle.

Tia Sandstrom Levings

Sustaining thought

Thank you for doing what you do and being who you are.

Day 12

Focus on Today

Today's understanding of your kids is good enough for today's lessons.

Don't try to figure out who they should be or become by year X. Focus on who they are today—what they present today—and learn alongside them, honoring and matching today's appetites.

Enough learning for tomorrow will happen today when you do just that.

Quote of the day

I love your thinking.

Poppy Troxel

Sustaining thought

Live and learn—along with your kids—one day at a time.

 Brave Writer

Day 13

It Gets Better

I'm not one for pie-in-the-sky platitudes (though clearly I'm okay with clichés). Being told that things will get easier, make more sense, or feel better in some time that is not now can feel like a pat on the head, not a rope thrown down a cliff.

But things will get better because you strive toward that end—that's who you are. You are a responsibility-taking initiator of "good things." I know this about you because you homeschool. That's the only kind of person who chooses this life.

I also know that you are an intrepid researcher because you homeschool. Those are the sort of people who take on the education of their children without degrees or training. They're the kind that tackle Big Huge Risky Tasks because they have such unswerving faith in their abilities—at minimum, their ability to research and apply what they need to know to achieve their ideals.

Oh, I know it doesn't always feel that way. Some days you feel like curling into a ball on a beanbag chair, sucking your thumb. Those days don't last too long, though, because you won't permit it.

You're the kind of person who after a few days of self-pity, looks into the mirror, gives yourself a pep talk, and re-ups the commitment. You most certainly do have that confidence. People without it don't homeschool.

This is the rope. Thrown down the cliff to you.

It's not a list of practices like breathing or running.

It's not a set of precepts about education and child development.

It's not the "perfect curriculum" that relieves you of the obligation to teach your children.

Nope.

The rope—*your* own tenacity and audacity. That's it!

Today's difficulty is merely one in a long string of challenges that you will attack with spirit and drive. Sure, it's not always rainbows and licorice in the middle of the muddle.

Of course not!

But you know that. You knew that when you started. It's like running: you know you'll get tired and out of breath. Well, here's that moment. Keep running.

At the core, you can trust that you will be better at this thing called homeschooling tomorrow than you are today. A year from now? Even better. You will get the hang of it.

Wait. I hear some of you say: "What if I never do get better at it? What if homeschool never feels happy or serene or satisfying the way I want it to be?"

 Brave Writer

Guess what I know you'll do? You'll figure out something else! Your drive to ensure a quality childhood for your children will leave you tireless in your pursuit of a better situation. You may have to change course. You may stop homeschooling after several years. Who's to say that is the wrong decision or an admission of failure? It might be the most powerful act of self-advocacy in your entire adult life!

I trust you! You can figure out what to do!

Here's what I know: homeschoolers are ethical, sincere, committed, hard working, optimistic, and resourceful.

That's you!

I trust your choices on the basis of those characteristics alone. Whatever you do, your life with your kids is going to get better and better (even through the messiness of teens or toddlers). That's how it works for parents like you.

Catch!

Grab the rope—it's you! You can pull yourself up, by your own strength of character. It will get better.

I've got cookies waiting for you at the top. See you there.

Quote of the day

> *I'm a teacher with a credential, and I still don't feel up to the task. I never imagined, in my wildest dreams, homeschooling. My plan was for my children to go to school! That plan failed miserably when my daughter,*

diagnosed with ADHD, came home from first grade
talking, every day, about how she wished she were dead.

After second grade, it was very obvious that I had
no choice, but to remove her or let them kill her.
Seriously! The second time around, I sent my son to
K. He came back saying what a bore it was. He was
displaying anger at not having the time with me
that his sister had. First grade rolled around, he was
assigned to the same teacher. There went the hope of
a more interesting year. So here I am, homeschooling
both. Crazy! I am attacking things with spirit and
drive, that's true. They are my children, after all.

Amy Wilson-Pineda

Sustaining thought

Homeschooling is a process, not a destination. You are
a conscientious person, and can be trusted to make good
decisions one day at a time for your family.

Day 14

It's the Context, Schweetheart!

If you need to turn a day around, change the environment. No lectures, no shaming sessions, no tongue-lashings, no careful explanations. Kids and teens respond to concrete experience, not abstract explanations and suppositions.

So, if you have cranky little guys, send them to jump it out on the trampoline. If you want them to learn their prepositions, act them out with a chair. If you've got a tired hand, cramped from holding a No. 2 pencil, hand the child a marker and a white board.

If the kitchen table is dull and uninspiring, write on a clipboard under the table.

If your teen drives, send her to the library or museum or local deli to study alone.

Sounds can change everything: play recordings of nature (rainfall, crackling fire, waves lapping the beach) during copywork. Use jazz music when cleaning up the family room (again!). Add salsa to bath time or lunch or art.

Create a centerpiece before math—scavenge rocks, pinecones, wildflowers, shells, moss on bark, driftwood—and ask your kids to arrange them, perhaps in geometric shapes. Maybe they can go in a triangle, then halfway through the lesson, your kids can rearrange them into another shape (circle), then at the completion of the lesson, a polygon!

Before the read aloud, face-paint. Pick an image or symbol from the book and put it on each child's cheek. Save writing (for a teen) for midnight and candlelight. Forbid writing until they are alone in the dark, with a single candle. See what happens.

Wear dress up clothes, allow ear buds for music, use a typewriter (if you have one), dress up the table, light a fire or sit outside on a blanket, study at a coffee shop, write at a nature center, make calculations at the grocery store, skip count in Spanish, use British accents for all school related activities for an afternoon...

Instead of writing, draw.

Instead of calculating with a calculator, use an abacus or measuring cups or rods.

Instead of reading aloud, use audiobooks—go for a drive!

Quote of the day

Love it! Julie, you and your team are amazing! Thanks for being such a blessing to so many!

Dana Roberts Brown

Sustaining thought

If your homeschool feels stale or you're in a rut, bring new energy to any subject area through refreshing the context of learning.

Day 15

Permission to Worry

I get emails: "When do I start to worry?" parents ask.

Aw yes, the question about worry—reworded it might sound like this:

"When do I have your permission to openly worry about my child's poor writing?"

If you are asking the question, you are already worrying. Let's just admit that right up front. Usually, though, some part of us knows that worry is counter-productive to a trusting happy relationship with our child. We also know that worry ratchets up our level of "schoolmarm-ish-ness." We become the tougher, harder, "time-to-get-serious" version of ourselves. The thing is, we don't really like her or him. We want to be the generous, optimistic, creative, relational teacher we imagine in our minds.

Until we have permission to worry, we do a number of things with our anxiety.

- We pretend it away.
- We cover it up with forced casualness.
- We ignore it.

- We shift our focus to the other children.

- We decide: "We'll just unschool this subject."

- We find support from other quarters to tell us that our kids are okay.

- We become tense and lose our ease of relating.

Our voices become tight and high-pitched. Then one day, we get to the end of our ability to "hold on." Perhaps a friend bragged about her child's writing. Perhaps you spent time with a schoolteacher who talked about what she requires of her students, same age as your child. Perhaps your mother asked you when she might see your child's writing.

Bam! You can't keep the worry down. So you want to know: "Can I admit how worried I am? Can I let that guilty feeling bubble to the surface and act on it?"

Permission to worry allows us to shed the guilt associated with becoming the "stern" parent. We feel justified in requiring more or expecting more. We aren't as sorry for losing the smile and insisting. We allow ourselves to be mobilized into action after that awkward extended period of quasi-patient waiting.

Rather than give you that permission, let me help you channel your worry (the worry already present, hiding behind your attempts to not worry) into productive action. Here are five things you can do with that worry, today!

1. Research

You can always google your little anxious heart into more information. Look up symptoms and read what you can about the issue. If it's writing, then by all means read, read,

 Brave Writer

read on the Brave Writer blog and website. But you might also benefit from reading about the childhoods of famous writers. Find out how many of them struggled and in what ways. Find out how professional writers solve writing problems. Get more information, rather than wringing your hands about phantom fears.

2. Test new practices

It's always a good time to try new approaches to a child's struggle. Go outside traditional education to find those strategies. For instance, if your child struggles with math facts, see if you can find practices used by accountants or cashiers that may shed a different kind of light on the issue (rather than doing endless curriculum research). Check out apps on the iPad or Tablet.

3. Triangle-in help

It's okay to hand off the struggle to an expert (tutor, therapist, best-friend-with-a-BA-in-said-subject, online class, co-op). Take a break and get a third person's help and perspective. It can help *enormously* to involve another party.

4. Take a break (set a date)

The hardest part of worry is doing nothing, but sometimes letting a child mature is the best thing you can do. To ease your guilt, set a date for how long you will conscientiously "do nothing." You might choose to ignore reading for three months before revisiting it. Put it on your calendar. If in the meantime, opportunities to support the task arise, enjoy them but don't latch onto them for dear life. Allow your "break" to be a real break.

5. Build trust

No child gets ahead in a difficult area without the support of a wiser, older, kinder person. You are that person. If reading or writing or math is particularly difficult for your child, work on building a good relationship in other easier areas. Make sure that you are enjoying art, taking walks, building Legos, reading great books, telling jokes, kicking the soccer ball, training the pet rats, learning magic tricks, etc. Do these with great love and energy, accommodating struggle, supporting challenge. As you do, you build a basis for continued work in the difficult areas. You might, accidentally, discover the issue that holds your child back in the other area. If you can create a loving bond in happy subjects, when you struggle to work on the difficult one, you will have a well of compassion and a bank of mutual regard to support you.

Worry if you must, but be productive with it. Don't dump it on your child, don't give yourself permission to become an old school marm, don't let your fear of failure as a home educator poison the beautiful homeschool life you are creating together.

You can't pretend worry away. Embrace it. Own it. Do something good with it.

Quote of the day

Thanks for sharing! I so needed to read this tonight!

Christie Radcliffe-Buelow

Sustaining thought

Give worry a big hug and then let it go.

© Julie (Bogart) Sweeney | bravewriter.com

Day 16

Keep Reading

In all our connectivity, we sometimes think we've read all day long, when in fact, we've absorbed bites of information as our eyes scroll over screens.

Read aloud time is one way to ensure that you get a dose of literature in your day. It nourishes you and your kids. It may take some work to find a way to fit it in (our family started the day with read aloud time, right after breakfast). But it's worth it. If you have wiggly toddlers or fussy babies, try to read to the older ones while the younger ones are napping or at the breast (if the baby tolerates it—some do, some hate it).

In addition to reading to the kids, though, I hope you will read for pleasure yourself. Consider it a part of your "teacher-training." You are a much better commentator on literature and movies when you, yourself, are reading adult fare. You are also a better human being when you connect to characters and their struggles/hurdles, and discover new resources for how to meet your own challenges. You are a happier person when your imagination is carried away to the tropics and a love story, or involved in solving the latest crime mystery.

Reading for pleasure may seem like a chore initially. Who has time for that?

Here are a few ways I found time when I was either pregnant, nursing, or both, and managing small children.

I read while I nursed a baby. This was my favorite way to read for years. Reading for pleasure while breast-feeding allowed me to rest both my mind and body.

I listened to books on tape while making dinner. The children watched the television show "Arthur" as I prepared the meal and enjoyed an adult story-time. This daily practice transformed how I felt about the end of the day.

I listened to many books on long car rides. When driving out of town, I would tackle Hemingway or Hugo or some other difficult to read book.

I used to read books aloud to my husband. We'd read a chapter before bed each night. We read some really long ones, including the entire Asia series by James Clavell (Shogun, Noble House, Taipan, and so on).

I kept a book in my purse (today you can use Kindle for the iPhone or bring your Kindle with you). All those visits to the doctor or dentist, sitting in a parked car during soccer or lacrosse practice, waiting for a performance to start for band or ballet—these moments are often crowded by cell phone scrolling now. But if you keep a book on your phone or if you tuck a paperback into your purse, you can read instead.

The benefits of reading are enormous. I recommend keeping one book going that is just for you. It's like giving yourself a big chocolate bar and eating a square of it each day. It's delicious, and you deserve it. Moreover, it makes you a better home educator and you'll hardly even realize why.

Quote of the day

I cannot imagine not reading for pleasure. I managed it even when my kids were little. My kids grew up seeing both my husband and me enjoy reading, which I think helped make them into readers.

Dawn Bouchard

Sustaining thought

Read for pleasure; read for learning; read for personal serenity.

Day 17

Of Trophies, Ribbons, and Medals

A popular theme in parent-discussion groups is to trumpet the lack of value of trophies, ribbons, and medals for participation in sports or the arts. The idea goes that if everyone gets one, no one earns one.

The thought is that kids need to learn that reward comes from achievement, that losses have a real impact on the outcome of a season or effort, and that the reception of a physical symbol for beating other teams (or perhaps, successfully performing to a higher standard that other performers) is meaningful/important, not rote, not cheapened by "everyone gets one."

Old-school parents trot out their memories of coaches who yelled; and practices that beat up their egos; and trophies they finally won; how worth it, it all was; and how they attained an impeccable character by only being rewarded for winning.

Winning proved that all that hard work and pain were worth it! The trophy told a story: these kids were better than everyone else. Their work was more impressive at the end. Beating people and having proof in the form of a trophy produced pride: this group of boys or girls could know that they stacked up as superior people, at least in this sport.

 Brave Writer

Not so fast, schweetheart.

Spare me the lectures about how soft this generation is becoming. We need to ask the obvious question: Is winning the goal of childhood activities? Should it be?

When I was 10 years old, I joined a swim team at our tennis club. Let's pause to appreciate that I was in a family who could afford swim team and a tennis club membership. Unlike the typical 10-year-old, I was small. As in tiny. My last name was "Sweeney" and I was called "Teeny Sweeney." The girls on this team ranged from ordinary girl to hefty. And then there was me.

Needless to say, in four years of competing, I never won a single race. Not one. I never even placed, unless you count "seventh" or "last." My times improved! I beat my own times repeatedly because I went to every practice and I tried hard. I had no ability to beat girls six inches taller than I was, however.

I finally quit the team in eighth grade. At my last meet, I won my heat in breaststroke (first time ever)! I would get the chance to swim for a ribbon! Oh wait—the loud speaker crackled to clarity—"Julie Sweeney is disqualified for improper strokes." My feet had come to the surface too many times. Of course. I couldn't have beat the other girls without that advantage. I slunk away from the blocks.

The last race of my illustrious career found me swimming the third leg of a relay race. If you know swimming, that is the slowest leg. Naturally, going into the third length of the pool, my team was in first place. Coming out of it, we were in fourth—thanks to my tiny body and short legs. The last swimmer had to make up for my lost time, and did, but we finished third—my one and only swimming ribbon to show for four years of swim team commitment.

I remember the drive home. I felt defeated. I wondered why I had bothered to swim at all. Sure, I had loved getting into a pool in the rain, sweating in the sauna, giggling with my buddies, licking dry green Jell-O out of the palms of my hands for energy before races, huddling under towels shivering and dripping wet, cheering for each other. But what was the point? I was a terrible swimmer because of my anatomy! I couldn't control that. I had failed.

Everything I controlled, I did well—showing up on time, wearing the right gear, trying really hard, applying the coach's advice, improving my speed and form, being a good teammate, taking criticism. "Nothing to show for it"—that's how it felt.

Of course, there was a lot to show for swimming. It was good for my health and my self-discipline. It was good to be on a team where I wasn't a star. When I was in gymnastics, I was the girl who got the good scores. In swimming, I learned humility, and what it was like to work hard even when I wasn't talented, or a part of the "best team." I learned to appreciate endurance sports. I became a competent swimmer—in pools, in the ocean. No small thing growing up in southern California.

I spent many happy hours in the pool, with friends, working hard, learning about my body and what it could be pressed to do beyond its natural aptitudes.

 Brave Writer

Would a pizza party and a little trophy at the end of my seasons have robbed me of those lessons? Would it have undermined how I understood achievement and accomplishment, and led me to a life of mediocrity?

Would a participation trophy have meant "nothing"?

I'd like to suggest the opposite! I might have been able to interpret my years on that team in a different light—in the light of commitment, hard work, and shared joy at my teammates' successes and struggles. I wish someone had said, "Great having you on the team. Thanks for participating!"

Children and teens should be encouraged to participate in all kinds of sports and activities, regardless of their natural acumen and aptitude. Why should piano only be for the prodigy? Why should baseball only be played by kids with great hand-eye coordination? What good is it to reduce all the effort and learning of playing sports to success on the field or in the pool or on the balance beam?

Why should any sports team for kids be about winning, frankly?!

Winning is a happy end result when several factors are in place:

1. Parents have money to spend on the sport. In some sports, the investment is significant!
2. Parents have time to coach, and know how to do it well.
3. The team winds up with a surprising collection of naturally gifted athletes.
4. The team "gels" and they get on a winning streak.

That only happens for one team per league. Literally.

Winning can't Be Everything. For kids, it should barely *be* a thing! Our children are growing—they are discovering how their bodies work, how to play hard, how to show up when they are cranky and hungry, how to take direction and practice skills, and how to adjust to new locations, other teams, and weather. Ninety-nine percent of our kids will not go on with any sport in college.

If we reduce a team's season's success to whether or not they got more wins than all the other teams, we are saying that all that effort that went into the sport is of no value. We are forgetting to honor and recognize the achievements that will build self-esteem (the real kind of self-esteem that comes from team play and hard work, not the kind that comes only from being the ones who "trounced" the other teams).

It's fine to give an "extra trophy" for winning—go ahead and make it good sized. It's equally (perhaps more) important to also honor the season's effort and commitment by the "losers." Trophies and pizza seem to be doing a good job, in my opinion.

Real life says that there is room for Coke and Pepsi. Heck, there's room for homemade sweet tea at the local diner, in addition to the big brand names. Not everything any of us does depends on a "will to win" or even "being the best." Sometimes being "not the best" is the best choice!

In fact, being a team player that loses graciously would be a fabulous outcome of a season. We could use more adults like that. As home educators, we give our children the gift

 Brave Writer

of valuing their growth, efforts, and curiosity every day—without grades, without measurements that tell them how they stack up with other kids. We do this because we've come to believe that their success as people doesn't depend on being better than others, but being the best people they can be, given their limits and talents.

Their milestones are worth celebrating. Their efforts deserve rewards and respect. Their achievements are respectable whether or not they are at the top of their field, class, grade level, or age. Why? Because their achievements are theirs.

If we teach kids to value their efforts and show them all that they learn when they participate with commitment and energy, besides "winning," we help them become people who build their self-understanding from the inside out (rather than outside-in).

They will not be dependent on others to tell them who they are. They will have a right, sober, honest perspective of themselves that they've built from the myriad experiences they chose to explore. That perspective will come from self-awareness, not a Championship Trophy.

That self-understanding is worth an Extra Large Pepperoni and a little gold statue in my book. At least that.

Quote of the day

...a little recognition goes a long way!

Bob

Sustaining thought

Order the Extra Large Pepperoni and celebrate the achievement of participation first.

Brave Writer

Day 18

Understand the Nature of Children

When it comes to parenting each of us is green—at first. There's no training, no practice run with pretend children. You are thrust into the love affair quite unprepared for the consuming demands on your time and heart, even if you've read a library's worth of parenting manuals in advance.

The twin tugs of our responsibility to raise a child "correctly" and our abject powerlessness in the face of a child's pain and struggle leave us ambivalent and self-doubting. Add the privilege and burden of home education to the mix, and you've upped the stakes one thousand percent!

As you fashion a philosophy and prepare your practices, your children defy you. They hate your organic, steamed, smashed vegetables that you grew in your garden, they refuse to sleep at convenient hours, they have an endless supply of giddy and slaphappy to express in quiet library lines and doctor's offices. They bait their siblings into tickle fights and then scream at you that their brother or sister is mean.

They ruin perfectly good toys—the ones they wanted for half a year. They leave a trail of food, plates, glasses, and half empty stale boxes of crackers—then complain that there are no clean dishes and nothing to eat (though you returned from the store an hour earlier).

Certainly they cuddle and surprise you with smiles and reward your care with endless entertainment. But the experience of ongoing "otherliness" that comes from parenting creates relentless low-level anxiety that we don't credit with depleting us. Yes we are physically tired. But we are also living with chronic chaos—nothing stays where it was put, and no child stays the same for long.

Just as you solve one problem or adapt to this stage of development, bam! The next one is ushered in, with all of its mystery and complexity.

Education—the balance between learning that comes naturally and from curiosity, and the skill-building that comes from direction and an awareness of what that child will need for a diploma or adult living—becomes the testing ground for your success as a parent.

Enter: frustration, exasperation, exhaustion, confusion, doubt, comparison, assessment, desperation, pressure, tears, arguments, battles, loneliness, fear, worry, and what feels like failure.

Children will lead you to the edge of yourself. Guaranteed. You will say what you promised you'd never say—and usually you'll shout those words.

You will require what you never expected to require. You'll forget love and feel loathing, and then loathe yourself for letting that feeling surface. The unfathomable tenacity of a child to resist what you have explained so well, so patiently, so clearly for his or her benefit, even with all your offers of help, will level you. Your feelings will be hurt!

 Brave Writer

How can this child not hear how much you want to help?

Why can't this child simply cooperate and try?

How can this request be *that* difficult? Really?

You will be unequal to the force of a child's unwillingness to do what you ask at some point in your parenting career. Not even spankings and groundings and lectures and the intimidation of a bigger parent will cause the child to reverse course.

The inevitable question follows: Now what?

When every offer of help is refused, when every punishment and reward fails, when you can't bring the mountain to Mohammed, what should you do? Where do you turn?

I suggest: perspective.

Sometimes the tears and the anger are a necessary part of the growth. Try not to take it personally. So she doesn't want to get dressed (and she's two years old!). This isn't about you; it isn't really about her. She's two! She's going to grow out of this exhausting phase. Some days you can skip dressing and leave her in her pajamas, and other days she will dress. On the days you have to leave the house, you will wrestle her into her clothes. With tears. With your own irritation fully available to you. And one day it will all stop. You'll look back and think, "Huh. I wonder when she decided to dress without drama?"

This same feeling applies to every area. With writing, it's much like this. We don't want to push to the point of tears and anger, but we do sometimes. I certainly lost it with Noah (he was the oldest, after all!). His resistance to being made to do what he didn't want to do is legendary in our family.

But time and again, with opportunity to grow, with calm conversations about what Noah needed for his future, combined with both moments of requirement and many more moments of easing the pressure, he emerged into his competent writing self, his mature wonderful adult self.

You will toggle! There may be a day where you are certain that writing must happen and your child will throw up an Armageddon of opposition. Do you battle through to eke out the words, and wind up exhausted and disheartened yet secretly glad you have something to show for English in your homeschool file?

Or instead, do you wave the white flag and make brownies, telling jokes, tickling him out of his mood? Do you stop writing altogether for a while until you get the nerve to bring it up again, hoping he'll mature out of this phase by then? Or do you simply do most of the work for him just to get it over with, and off your back?

Yes.

All of the above. That's what parenting looks like. You will do all of these.

Brave Writer

Some magic fairy comes along as the years unwind, and combines these acts with the sincerity of your love for and enduring commitment to that child, and turns it all into an education and a relationship. Memories come from this magical combination. A lifetime of healthy, happy and whole is possible from these raw parenting excursions. You are learning as you go. Give yourself some grace to push, to pull back, to try again, to do too much, to not help enough. In that mix, with this child, you will find a groove. It's not too late (never too late). It's okay to put stuff on hold and let it be for a good while. It's also okay to push at times when you know it's the right thing to do.

I remember I wouldn't let Jacob quit saxophone lessons because I knew he'd love marching band in high school. Since he was homeschooled and not in a band, he had no way of knowing he'd love it so he got bored with lessons. But I knew differently. I knew he would love marching band and kept him going with lessons despite his resistance. I was right. He was glad. In the end.

This is parenting—the push, the pass over, the support, the help, the letting go, the requirement, the acceptance. You're doing it right, if you are doing all of this, and asking the questions, and modifying your practices, and paying attention to your connection to your children.

You are! Don't let anyone tempt you into thinking there's one right way. We try it all, and then...

...keep going.

Quote of the day

Woman, please call me every morning (or maybe every afternoon when my head is exploding), and say things like this to me. I will pay you. In chocolate.

Brianna McLeod Preston

Sustaining thought

When you feel like you're at the end, be gentle with yourself, and keep going.

Day 19

Whatever Works for You, Do It!

You know your kids and your personality. You get to decide what you like or don't like, what programs work or don't work for your family. Anyone who knows me or has spent time with Brave Writer is well aware that I'm not out to convince you to change what you are doing if it satisfies and works for you.

My objective is to promote a specific vision of writing. It's not the only vision of writing. It is my vision of writing and it's one I've cultivated for 30+ years. It comes from a wide variety of sources (academic and professional, personal and exploratory). I've worked in the popular writing market and I've had success in academic writing contexts, both. I've spent countless hours (thousands) working with families and adults who want to be better writers.

The main purpose of Brave Writer, all the way back to before the beginning, has been to give parents tools to bridge the gap between their children's lively conversation and their stilted writing results. This exasperating experience is common to all writing instructors.

Entire educator conferences are devoted to finding ways to solve this dilemma in the classroom. Writer's Workshop is one of the most well-known educational tools/programs that approximates the kind of work Brave Writer teaches, but its appropriate context is the classroom (which has its own peculiarity since there are other subjects to teach, student-teacher ratios are higher than parent-to-child ratios at home, and there are academic achievement measurements to satisfy).

Still other programs break writing down into more steps, on the assumption that if they provide tools and skill in the mechanics first, thought will flow more freely due to confidence in transcription skills. These tools include imitating great writing, applying a set of concepts to the writing (talking about sentence variety and how to raise the eloquence of the "speech-like" drafting to the more sophisticated sound of written language), and putting spelling and grammar programs first.

For many students and parents, the relief that comes from being told what to do, step by step, is enormous after failure and insipid, weak drafting. I've seen some families thrive or blossom through this approach. It is not morally wrong! It is not objectively bad. For many, it is a way forward and for some (particularly for natural writers), it's a joy to play with the puzzle of writing in new, directed ways.

If this approach were sufficient, however, schools and writing programs would all adopt it and our children would happily apply those steps and concepts and become the writers we hope they will be. But that isn't what happens. A large number of children (and adults) are unhappy writing that way. They are not able to connect their personhood to the writing—writing feels external to them in that system.

 Brave Writer

Some children may weather the tedium/challenge of the step-by-step approach to get to the "good stuff" where they find their voices. But a large number don't get there. In fact, they feel stifled and bored, angry and tearful.

How do I know this? I work with these kids. We've had countless families come to Brave Writer when their children are at the end of their wits—so blocked and resistant, they don't ever want to write again. For some reason, the attempt to make the writing process easier through understanding the mechanics first doesn't create enthusiastic writers for many kids (and adults).

Lots of them need to know that what they are writing is meaningful to them before they care about the structure, forms, or mechanical details. To risk the mess that comes from attending to the inner life of a child first takes courage! Parents worry that they will encode bad habits and poor spelling, or that they will teach their children that forms and editing don't matter.

But what turns out to be true is that when kids get excited about their ideas and thoughts, when they know that what lives inside is worthy of the page, it is far easier (in many many contexts) to be interested in the mechanics and structure of writing. That's what I've found. That's what professional writers know. That's what loads of academics are now saying about how to teach writing in college...and on down as the insights trickle to the lower levels of school.

That's what many of you have told me.

That's what lots of parents have discovered.

Do you have to jettison the writing programs you've already purchased? Of course not! Once you discover how to nurture and nourish your child's writing voice, you may find numerous ideas and tools to help enhance and enrich the output. I use a wide variety of tools myself when I write, not just one. Being able to adapt to different teaching styles is also a valuable experience for teens, in particular, as they prepare for the variety of demands of college professors.

The bottom line is this: I will promote and protect this space for the writing philosophy that Brave Writer advocates. That philosophy is too often misunderstood or critiqued as not being rigorous or being for "creative writing only." Parents who take the risk to embark on this program need support so that they can trust the process and not be waylaid by guilt or anxiety that they are "doing it wrong." Usually the thrill they experience when their formerly blocked writers take to the page is sufficient, though.

Happily.

Even so, you must be brave to follow this philosophy when everyone else is following systematic programs with rubrics and rules. I want to reassure you that we address it all in Brave Writer (grammar, format, creativity), just in a different order than traditional models.

Not only that, I want to add: we live in the 21st century, in a globalized world of published writing (twitter, Facebook, comments on news articles, blogs, online journals, texting, and more). Writing strategies have necessarily evolved—we live in a world that requires us to value all

 Brave Writer

kinds of writing voices, even less educated ones, even ones with an "accent," even ones that fail to spell correctly or type beautifully, even ones that hold diametrically opposed beliefs and values to our own.

To me, the most gracious thing we can do as readers is to hear the content before we rush to judgment over form and format, grammar and spelling. Let's give each other that gift and make the world safe for writing risks.

Thank you for your participation and for your wonderful contributions of what works in your families.

Quote of the day

> *Brave Writer was probably the most important purchase of my year. It changed the way I homeschool, affecting all my other subjects. Kids love it, I love it, and I will continue to use it for years and years.*
>
> *R Burke*

Sustaining thought

We give our children a gift when we pay close and caring attention to the content of their writing.

Day 20

Don't Trust the Schedule

Scheduling is a necessary tool for dental appointments, piano lessons, and date nights.

It is less useful for homeschooling. Here's why.

When you create a schedule, you attempt to control time in a space designed for "escape from time." Home is where we let go, let down, and live in a relaxed, un-hurried, no pressure state. It's where we go to get away from time's demands. We unconsciously unwind at home (or at least, we certainly want to unwind at home).

Along come your "school-at-home" notions, built from your memories of traditional schooling; we bring the clock and bell into this relaxed, "be myself" environment. We decide to structure things like breakfast and teeth-brushing so that we can "start" the school day.

We try to monitor the length of time spent in one subject area so we can move to the next. We manage naps for babies and DVDs for toddlers to free time for the focused attention our olders need. We pick a time for lunch and try to hit it consistently.

Some parents are brilliant schedulers, and make this uncomfortable fit of time measurement and home, work.

© Julie (Bogart) Sweeney | bravewriter.com   Brave Writer

But for those who fail (or believe they are failing), there's a good reason for it. Not only do your children resist being marshaled to accommodate the artificial imposition of time constraints on home activities, but at some level, so do you.

You know it's artificial.

You do answer the telephone or respond to a text in the middle of the math lesson.

You do sleep in some days when the baby kept you up all night.

You are likely to flop on the couch and take a micro nap after the read aloud, because you literally can't stay awake.

You walk around in pajamas long after breakfast, and suddenly remember you need to go online to pay a bill or reserve a space or change an appointment.

Home is a fabulous space because you actually can do all those things! You can't in an office. You certainly can't in a school!

Home is that place where you maneuver through the waves of activity like a skiff—quick, sharp turns, at full speed. You aren't an ocean liner, needing ample warning to avoid icebergs, monitoring every engine, taking huge quantities of time to make small adjustments. You are navigating your day freely, weaving and bobbing around the interruptions, taking advantage of an open sea of time when it arises, and then shutting it all down when three out of four kids get sick. You do this even after you've created a schedule! That's what's so odd. You know that you aren't truly tied to that schedule, which is why you violate it.

If you are living (and dying) by a schedule, sick children produce resentment: they are messing with your project for efficiency!

If you live by a schedule, the day you sleep in means you are behind all day (when I'm behind all day, I'm not as nice a mother or person).

The conflict between home and schedule can be resolved by dumping the schedule and admitting the nature of home.

Home is a space where each person has a certain amount of freedom to just "be." Within that "beingness," it's possible to learn an enormous quantity of information. That's why we brought our kids home from traditional schooling—we believed that the homey-ness of home was not antithetical to learning. Rather, we believe that home is even more conducive to learning than school with its clocks and bells.

That's because it happens to be true: tutorial-based, interest-driven, time-unbound learning is effective—supremely so.

Home creates a space for that kind of learning to flourish. Why ruin it with a schedule?

What I propose is the homeschool routine. Rather than trying to schedule the days, set up a routine (a spare one—with a few reliable practices) that can be returned to when you have "one of those days." Follow inspiration whenever possible. She is not a lengthy visitor.

 Brave Writer

But on the rest of the days, we can know that after we wake up, we eat breakfast (no matter how early or how late in the morning). After breakfast, we move to the family room for read aloud and I read until we are finished (a single chapter or four, depending on the mood and happiness of the family).

After reading, we do copywork (at least a couple days a week). We pick the days based on everyone's energy level for writing (if it's a heavy writing day, we don't do copywork in addition). We move to math after reading and writing. The math pages are chosen based on progress and effort. If a child struggles with a concept, then more time is given with fewer problems to solve. If the concept is easy, the page is completed quickly and perhaps only alternating problems assigned.

An on-going history lesson or project follows lunch, picking up where we left off before (no assigned pages, no "place to get to by the end of February" in mind). History can continue this way...forever. Who said there's a certain amount you must finish by June? My family got stuck in Ancient Greece and Egypt for two years. We loved it! We wanted to camp there.

Perhaps you have other library books to read to the little kids (picture books) later in the day. These are done before naps, as many as everyone wants.

Other activities can be included in the routine (scrapbooking, the Red Herring series, Tuesday Poetry Teatimes, an ongoing game, computer play, Rosetta Stone, birding, building a model, art and piano lesson practice). But each of these is given time (without a constraint) to be done as the child has the capacity to sustain interest.

It's nearly impossible to schedule energy and interest level. That's why school feels dull so frequently. The assigned hours have nothing to do with a student's attention span, curiosity, energy to perform well, and the peacefulness of the atmosphere. Regardless of how a student feels, he or she is expected to perform in hard chairs, with small desks, surrounded by others, facing a teacher who is examining their eyes for attentiveness, while (perhaps) remembering being bullied at recess.

At home, kids have the benefit of being themselves. They can make themselves comfortable—lying prone on the floor, lounging on the couch, sitting at the kitchen island. Of course this kind of freedom produces two effects: keen concentration and absolute sloughing off! Both occur when we are allowed to "be" rather than feeling pressure to "perform."

We create the conditions of excellence and quality performance when we honor the rhythms of life at home, when we value the hot white fire of passion when we see it (rather than remarking, "But that's not on the schedule today"). We sustain growth when we return to the comfort of the routine when all other energies are subdued. And we honor our human frailty if we toss routine, schedule, or structure when we are falling apart (sick, irritated, frustrated, in pain, exhausted, or bored).

   Brave Writer

Schedule is tempting. It holds the promise of "getting it all done" which we translate into our heads as "completing our children's education." Don't be seduced by that promise. Mostly what I hear from parents under the pressure of schedule is "I'm behind" and "I feel like a failure" and "I'm terrible at staying on schedule."

Of course you are. You're at home. Be home. Embrace the properties of home. Love. Live. Be. Learn. Thrive.

We're so lucky to be home. The best gift you can give your family is to be glad that you are, and to live as though home is the ideal space for learning to occur. Because it is.

Quote of the day

Oh Julie, thank you, thank you, thank you. I so needed this tonight. I have been putting off creating yet another schedule/checklist and couldn't concretely understand why I was resisting. You nailed it. I want to add one more tidbit to your profound post. I just saw this quote on Pinterest: "Focus on what you have accomplished rather than beating yourself up over what you have not."

Ginger Padgett

Sustaining thought

Homeschools thrive on a blend of inspiration and routine, while you make adjustments freely as needs arise. Trust the properties of life at home: freedom, space, time, and love.

Day 21

Invest 30 Minutes in the Morning

If you spend 30 minutes with your kids right after breakfast, you will be free for the rest of the morning.

Pick an activity that you want to do (painting a bedroom, repotting your indoor house plants, baking cookies, peeling wallpaper in the ugly bathroom, figuring out how to hook up the new game console, cleaning out one closet, washing the camping equipment, reorganizing the cupboards, weeding the garden, watering the flowers, laundry) and involve your kids with you.

Give assignments to everyone. Even the youngest child can help by dancing to music to entertain you while you read instructions for the IKEA bookcase you want assembled. It is a slower process when doing the activity with your kids. But it's even more difficult to distract them long enough to finish it without their "interference."

You can circumvent the whole struggle by including them at the get-go. They love grown-up activities, they love to be needed, and they can do more than you think (though more slowly, with less proficiency). They will find themselves interested and learning while you get through this important task.

At a certain point, their enthusiasm or energy will fade (they are kids and care less about repotting houseplants than you do). They will leave you to continue while they do something else.

 Brave Writer

And even if they don't, if they need to shift activities and you must come with them, at least you will have invested 30 minutes in that project and you will have moved the chains another ten yards down the field.

If you invest 30 minutes right after breakfast, you prevent a build up of resentment, too. You won't keep hoping for that "slip of time" when they are happy and you can get to work. Instead, you will set the agenda for the day by including everyone up front. You'll get some of it done (or a lot).

Most important, you'll eliminate resentment (waiting for them to be happy so you can work; waiting for you to finish so they can have a playmate).

Quote of the day

Awesome advice!! I'm going to do it!

Scott Johnson

Sustaining thought

A half hour each morning is all it takes to get things rolling!

Day 22

It's the Process, Baby!

Repeat after me: process, not product.

> *Education is an Atmosphere, a Discipline, a Life.*
> —Charlotte Mason

Let's notice what Charlotte did not say.

She did not say:

"Education is meeting the requirements of the Common Core."

She did not say:

"Education is the successful achievement of degrees—first high school, then college, then graduate school if you have a true education."

She also did not say:

"Education is mastering Reading, Writing, and Arithmetic."

Moreover, she did not say,

"Education is what someone does to you by teaching Important Information through tests, and grades."

Instead, Charlotte tells us to take our eyes off "end points" and to focus on creating a rich life through

Brave Writer

shaping the atmosphere (environment), through discipline (intentionality—being conscious of learning opportunities, creating them, acting on them), through life itself (the process of being alive is our best classroom).

You are on the right track when you get off track and focus instead on the feel of your home and family vibe. Ensure that people feel heard, loved, and that their dreams and hopes matter and can be achieved.

You're on the right track when you ebb and flow—some weeks making a "course of study" a priority in a systematic way, other weeks learning as you go, guided by curiosity and enthusiasm.

You're on the right track when you see all of life as your classroom—the conversation about recycling plastic bags over bagels at breakfast is as important as the math pages completed before lunch.

No one "arrives" at an end point: Time stamp—*educated*. Rather, we have intermittent markers that let us pause to appreciate this new place (graduated, finished a book, learned to read, understood a principle and can use it). The purpose of education, though, is to *live* a *life*—not to idolize the mastery of facts, figures, and theories.

That's why I return to this mantra: *It's the process, baby*. If you can let go of your need to match the state's expectations, or your schoolish memories, or the pressure of your very academic classical homeschool community, or the stringent requirements of some important university, you can surf the waves of learning as they roll onto your shores.

For example:

You'll feel freer to put vintage dance lessons (and the work you do to barter for them, maybe even with the kids along) ahead of history for that one period of six months. The learning is in all of it—the lessons, being with adults, the history of dance, the bartering work to pay for the lessons, the music, being in the cultural center of our local community, borrowing the fancy gown for the ball, participating in the ball, watching Jane Austen films over and over again to see which dances they are performing and which ones are being learned at class, manners, exercise, being paired with a sibling and learning to work together and building a solid, loving relationship.

Atmosphere: dance lessons, with adults who are passionate about preserving historical dance.

Discipline: weekly lessons, must memorize steps and practice, weekly distribution of flyers to pay for lessons.

Life: siblings dancing together, community supplying costumes for ball, family attending the ball to see how the two students mastered the dances, attending rehearsals with all five kids, distributing flyers with all five kids to pay for two kids, watching and learning by being in the room with the dancers, being a family that loved vintage dance.

See?

Did dance go on a single transcript anywhere? No. Yet vintage dance still ranks as one of our top educational experiences during the homeschooling years. *And* no one

 Brave Writer

still dances! The kids moved on—because it's the process, baby. Onto the next atmosphere, discipline, and life.

Quote of the day

Wow! I LOVE how you listed them out under the categories of atmosphere, discipline, and life. We aim at these but I can't wait to show the kids when and how we hit the target by listing them! Thank you for that little tweak that totally transformed.

Tracey

Sustaining thought

Revise your understanding of learning so that you can support your children in exploring their passions, even if those passions are eventually retired.

Day 23

Be Responsive

I heard from a mom this morning who may remind you of you. She is ping-ponging between structure and freedom, routine and wide open spaces of happy, invested "wasted" time. The back and forth swing feels unnerving—like she should have picked one or the other by now, and what should she do about two kids—one who feels comforted by the predictable pattern, and the other who collapses into tears of frustration in the face of assigned pages?

The way most parents handle this predicament is to try lots of ideas—looking for that one right fit that takes everyone into account. Me too! I'm just like you.

My journey included principles gleaned from the following streams of home education, mostly in this order. I started in 1991.

KONOS (kinesthetic unit-studies—wonderful!)

Roger and Dorothy Moore's approach to learning math and reading in the early years (love them)

Ruth Beechik's ideas about copy work and dictation (genius)

Sonlight (literature-based history and language arts; I was there the day SL was born!)

    Brave Writer

Other reading lists and literature-based programs I discovered at conventions, through friends, and at the library.

The Internet (watershed event of my life). Now I had lots of people to talk to about homeschooling and my choices expanded again.

Charlotte Mason (both freedom and form, living books and getting out of doors, art, a lifestyle, tea; spent five years with a terrific Charlotte Mason group in Dayton which shaped a lot of my thinking about learning and loving)

Classical Education (for the categories—logic, grammar, rhetoric; for the book lists; for the style of inquiry)

Delight-directed learning (following a child's passions and letting those expand to include what needs to be learned)

BHAGs (Big Hairy Audacious Goals; a business management term—catching sight of a child's big dreams and shaping the education to suit them, supporting the process to bring them to life)

Unschooling (hands off! let them go! put away textbooks!)

The Teenage Liberation Handbook (meant much more to me than my kids since they had never been in school—it helped to deschool me, to give me courage to risk with Noah as a teen)

Radical unschooling (being attentive to my child and coordinating that with opportunities, deep appreciation for how learning happens from within and how to be a parent who is engaged enough to facilitate it and stand in awe of it)

Re-enter Textbooks (some subjects benefitted from use: science, math—I had the courage to go there, and it took courage)

Tutors (math, SAT prep, art, piano, saxophone, sewing, handwriting therapy for dysgraphia, speech therapy)

Classes and camps (co-op, local high school, zoo, vintage dance, online courses, Shakespeare acting, space camp, marching band, color guard, theater, poetry club at the library)

Public School (some part-time, some full time high school)

College

The inputs from each of these streams created the education we called homeschool. I did not pick one philosophy and stick to it for all 17+ years—who can? You don't know what you are doing…you have to figure it out as you go. It's hogwash to think that if you didn't find the right stream early enough, you will never find your way. Your kids are getting an education, but so are you! You're growing as an educator, as a learner, as an adult, and as a parent. You didn't come into homeschooling whole and ready to go. You jumped in—expecting that you could educate your children while you learned how to given them an education. So amazing! What courage!

Give yourself space and time to change your mind, to course correct, and to feel okay about your lack of certainty.

Not only that: I didn't stop being a home educator just because some of my kids went to high school. I edited papers, discussed ideas brought up in class, read textbooks

 Brave Writer

to help with comprehension, set up tutors, helped with the adjustment to school, and more. In some ways, I felt as though I were homeschooling public high school. It was our joint big project!

Oddly enough, even the homeschool lifestyle continues to this day with my adult children.

When the grown-up kids come home, we still drink tea, read poetry, play word and board games, speak foreign languages to each other, read books together at coffee houses in each other's company, recommend books, talk about feminism, genocide, North Korea, social work, politics, and favorite authors; we play cards, watch both documentaries and popular movies, share music and discuss it, and still notice birds and art.

If you value learning together with your children, homeschool is not a task you complete one day and then you're done. Rather, it is an ongoing source of relationship and self-education that your family will share throughout their lives.

All the choices you make shape who you become to each other.

It's okay that you didn't find the right system earlier. There is no right system!

There is you, your family, and what you stumble upon that helps you each year as you move forward in life.

Promise yourself one thing, and I think you'll be okay:

Stay responsive.

Stay responsive to the moment (what's working, what isn't?)

Stay responsive to the child (what's working for this child, what isn't?)

Stay responsive to new input (don't disqualify any educational idea or tool because you are afraid you will look bad to some group of homeschoolers)

Stay responsive.

Allow your homeschool to evolve, morph, grow, or shrink (if it needs to). Be strong and courageous to stick up for your choices in the face of pressure to feel badly about them. Do not adopt a system, or a set of values and beliefs that trump the individuals who live in your home.

There is no right system.

There is only your family. Love them, pay attention to them, and try lots of ideas (taste them like you were at the Taste of Cincinnati and walking down the long hot walk way sampling Belgian waffles, beers, and bratwursts—a little of this and a little of that). Be satisfied with your unique blend of quality ideas that you sift and apply to your family, trusting that all together, you will have created a life that values learning.

If you ever feel belittled or shamed about the choices you make for your family, leave that group. Once you feel pressure to conform, you can't be responsive to your family— you will substitute the system—for love.

Protect your family from judgment. Stand up for yourself. Learn. Enjoy.

    Brave Writer

Quote of the day

I love this! It describes my family and our homeschooling adventure perfectly. Thank you! Just what I needed to start off a new semester.

Amy Boyd

Sustaining thought

Never let a system for education replace love for individuals.

Day 24

Teach Self-Awareness

We spend a lot of time on the 3 Rs and creating a happy, invested learning life with our kids. We show them household skills like wallpaper stripping and toilet-bowl scrubbing.

The chief skill we need to impart for successful relationships in life is self-awareness. I define self-awareness as: "the ability to know your thoughts, feelings, and needs; and then to take care of them yourself."

We blame others when we don't have self-awareness. We lash out at the nearest person, expecting the unsuspecting, kind bystander to take care of the agitation suddenly erupting inside. For instance, a hungry child may grab your pant leg and whine, "Mommy, I don't want to go to the store" when really he means, "Mommy, I need a cup of Cheez-Its."

An older child, humiliated in defeat, just beaten by long-distance competitors in World of Warcraft, may suddenly yell at a sibling: "Turn down the television! I hate that show!"

The thing that evokes the anger or whining is often a cover for what's really going on. We don't want to know ourselves because if we do, we must act for our own good. We wrongly assume that it feels better to get someone else to act for us.

 Brave Writer

One way to foster self-awareness in family members is to have it yourself. Narrate your own self-inquiry and self-care.

"These shoes littering the hallway are driving me crazy! Wait. I just realized that I'm trying to think of how to coordinate Sarah's dress rehearsal with Sam's soccer match and these shoes are distracting me from thinking of a solution. I feel like yelling!"

It isn't always natural to narrate your inner life, but it is helpful when you do. You can also help your children develop self-awareness.

"I see you don't want to go to the store. Are you hungry? Can I make you a turkey sandwich, first, and then we'll see if you want to go?"

"Whoa! That's a huge reaction to the TV. What happened? Did something 'not good' happen in your game?"

Eruptions are usually what happen to us when we aren't attending to the build-up of stress and anxiety inside. We aren't honest with ourselves. We're hungry, tired, worried, fearful, insecure. Instead, we blame the nearest intrusion as the reason for our 'agitation.'

Pause, help your child (and yourself!) take responsibility for the panicky explosion. Learn how to self-soothe, how to provide self-care.

I remember when Jacob was a toddler, he'd get worked up into a near-tantrum state. He'd then leave the room and go cry on his bed. When he was finished, he'd come back into the room cheery and ready to play. Pretty high self-awareness for a two-to-three-year old!

Help your kids understand how to take themselves out of the room/activity while they figure out what's going on inside. There's nothing wrong with being heartbroken about losing a game or annoyed that trips to the store are preventing lunch. Knowing that is what's going on is key to family harmony.

Quote of the day

Julie- I'm starting to wonder if you have a little "spy camera" into our home! Your posts have been so "spot on" with what's going on here and trials we are facing, and things we need to work on! Thank you so much for sharing your wisdom with others who need to hear it!

Nanci Smith

Sustaining thought

The invisible curriculum of a home education is the gift of self-awareness.

© Julie (Bogart) Sweeney | bravewriter.com Brave Writer

Day 25

Three Fail-Safe Activities to Bust Boredom

Boredom does not automatically create the conditions for creativity. More often it creates conditions for poking, tickling, nagging, arguing about the TV and computer, and needless fussbudgeting.

Don't be trapped by this myth that if you leave kids alone long enough, they'll turn into mini Steven Spielbergs producing films in your backyard!

Creativity is catalyzed by materials that inspire the imagination. Children are concrete thinkers. That means they need tactile involvement, not ideas to contemplate. They don't create ideas from the thin air inside their brains. They create from a pile of Legos, or sticks, or watercolor paintbrushes. If they can't find the tools, if they are told to go get the tools, if they are asked to put in the effort to create the conditions for creativity, they will often give up before they start.

Perhaps you've noticed: If you tell a child, "How about painting? You love painting," and the paints are hidden in a cupboard, no painting is going to happen. Rather, you might notice a bored child. Then without talking, walk to the cupboard; remove the paints and brushes and blank white paper. Set them on a cleared table in the same room where you are. Fill a glass with water. Sit at the table and begin to paint. Say nothing. You only have to paint for two or three minutes. I promise. Within that time, someone in the bored cluster of children is going to join you. Once that happens, you are nearly there. Boredom is about to wave the white flag. When you see the energy rise to take up this activity, you can then separate yourself by a short distance (stay in the room, ooh and ahh, offer suggestions, be enthusiastic about all attempts, and add brownies or snacks). You may be able to resume the work you were doing once the engine of creativity gets rolling.

1. Painting is nearly always a winner because it involves one of the three secret boredom-busting weapons: Water. When in doubt, add water. Water play changes everything. Toddlers can be tossed into a bathtub or a literal tub. When I lived in Morocco, we used washtubs for play. You can do that with a small wading pool. Put it right in the middle of your kitchen floor. Fill it about 6-8 inches deep. Dump all your measuring spoons and cups into the middle. Add sponges, squirt bottles, squirt guns, rubber ducks, and if your kids are grimy, a little bubble-bath liquid. Swish with your hands. Indoor water play is magical—on a waterproof surface, under your watchful eye, you can be in the kitchen/family room space doing what you need to do while small ones are happy.

Older kids also love water play. Invest in Super Soakers or sprinklers. Pull your car into the driveway and supply your kids with all the tools to wash your car. The key to making this fun and not a chore is being sure there are cool products to use on the car that soap it up, that squeegee the windows,

 Brave Writer

and so on. Loud music and friends make this activity more fun too. Reward with a trip to an ice cream shop.

Naturally, painting furniture/pictures/flower pots (rinsing brushes in water), writing on the driveway with water and paintbrushes, swimming in a pool, washing windows, Slip 'N Slides, wading in a creek, walking in the rain with umbrellas, splashing in puddles and curbside gutters. These are all magnetic experiences for kids.

The key, though, is beginning the activity without any words. You start it. You do it. Say NOTHING. No suggestions, no telling the kids to go outside and play with water. That doesn't work with bored kids. They need to see the option in action and you are the person to do it! Get it started and then see what happens.

2. If water is not an option, creating hidey-holes usually is. Blankets, sheets, towels, cardboard boxes, small pieces of movable furniture. The second surefire boredom buster is creating forts! Think outside of your usual "sheet over a card table" idea. You might create one on your deck. Tack a blanket or sheet across the hand railing in a corner (the blanket will be triangular over the space). Put cushions underneath with soft throws and a little low side table. Include a basket with books to read. You might even create a private entrance based on how you arrange the top sheet.

Forts behind couches, in the corner in your kitchen, behind a big recliner in the living room, in the basement, in your master bedroom (feels special to be in there! Never forget that). Bring snacks once it's created.

3. The most overlooked surefire boredom buster creates more work for you. I suggest you prepare this one ahead of time and save it for the day when you are at wit's end and need something that will absolutely change the tone of the home: a treasure hunt!

The trick is to get the cards in place because your kids can't watch you. So you may need to distract them with food or TV or time outside (you can say, "I need you to not come into the room where I am because of a top secret mission. I will tell you when it's safe to return").

Any use of the word "secret" will yield you big-time trust points with your kids. The treasure hunt can be as lengthy and elaborate as you like, but easy clues and simple treats work just as well. Here are a few ideas to get you started.

- Put the clues on note cards. Keep a list of the clues and where you will hide them so you can help kids who get stuck finding the next clue.

- The clues can rhyme but don't have to. For small children not yet reading, a sketch or photo is just fine! They can match the picture to the next location. Another idea is to use word scrambles for the clues. Or a clue could be a task they must complete before you give them the answer for where to look next. For instance, you might have a clue that says, "Hop on the left foot 10 times, then I'll release the next clue." Or you might have one that says, "Get the mail from the letter box, bring it to me, then I'll give you the next clue."

 Brave Writer

- Be careful not to use this activity as a disguised way to get chores done (kids are smart!). But you could include a mixture of silly activities (reciting tongue twisters, looking up a famous saying online, doing a back bend) with household benefitting activities (put away three pairs of shoes, brush your teeth, return the DVDs to their right cases).

- You want more than 3-5 clues or the game will end too quickly. Kids do great with 8-10 clues. Too many gets wearying, especially if the clues are difficult to solve.

- Consider treats midway through the treasure hunt. It's fun to get partway there and then know that you have been rewarded for that. A plate of grapes, a pair of stickers, a pack of gum, a super ball or pick-up sticks make good midway treats.

- The final item to be found ought to be worth the hunt. I recommend a brand new board game—something no one has played yet. A new DVD works, as does any artsy-crafty activity. Maybe a new water gun (cycling back to the #1 boredom buster)!

To review, when kids are bored turn to:

1. Water

2. Forts

3. Treasure Hunts

See how it goes! Remember—the secret to success is your involvement in the initial phase without *any* words. No words. No urgings, no suggestions, no lectures, no explanations, no hints.

Start the activity on your own and see who joins you. Even the treasure hunt—you can pull the first index card from a pocket and say, "Hmmm. I wonder what this means" and read it aloud. Then see who joins you to solve it.

Good luck!

Quote of the day

I need to make room for 'play days' for us to refresh us, revive us. It will fortify us to keep on keeping on. Thanks!

Nanci Smith

Sustaining thought

Lead your children into adventures by example—act, rather than talk. See who follows, and enjoy the process.

© Julie (Bogart) Sweeney | bravewriter.com   Brave Writer

Day 26

To Plan or Not to Plan Your Lessons

One of the greatest pleasures in life is to have someone else prepare a pleasurable experience for you. For instance, when I eat dinner at someone else's home, the food tastes better, the whole experience is elevated to "special," and I find myself relaxed and happy before the dinner begins, simply in anticipation.

Don't get me wrong. I enjoy making a quality meal too. The tinkering with the ingredients, the paging through the cookbook, the skillful braising and simmering and broiling—these all help me invest in the meal, and I love the feeling of being a confident, competent cook. Still, even though I have taught myself to cook, and have enjoyed the effects of my cooking, I absolutely love meals cooked for me—whether at a friend's home or a restaurant. There's a different kind of happiness that comes from that experience.

Home education also benefits from these two modalities of learning: the first kind—self-teaching to become a competent student of any subject area, and the second kind—benefiting from the well-prepared lesson offered by a caring parent.

In toggling between independent learning (the kind a child initiates and continues on his own) and lessons (the kind organized by you), your child will become a well-rounded, educated person. He'll have the power and skill to teach himself (such a gift!), but he'll also receive the gift of a lesson well prepared.

Self-guided instruction is a popular motif in home education. It's one of its fabulous goals, too. Anyone who realizes that a little concerted effort and a willingness to explore/read/test ideas without the badgering of a schedule or a series of pop quizzes and tests, discovers the joys of being an autodidact. We love that our kids can and do teach themselves all manner of subjects and skills.

What about the other end, though? While our goals may be to create independent learners, we might also want to consider how especially pleasurable it can be to learn according to a carefully considered plan that a parent puts together with love. I'm not talking about lectures and note taking. I'm talking about a plan—preparing in advance which books to read and how they will be read (aloud in a group or to oneself), considering field trips that might be coordinated with the books, assembling materials for art or science projects that correlate with the time period of the books, identifying music or artwork from that era in history that could be shared to enrich the experience of the reading and exploring, and so on.

In other words, one of the most generous acts you can offer as a home educator is a well-thought-out course of study in at least one subject area each quarter for the coming school year. It may be difficult to give that level of development to every subject for all ages, but you can certainly select literature or an historical time period that will address most of your children.

     Brave Writer

You can coordinate various activities, readings, outings, and related experiences that will illuminate some aspect of the subject area you intend to explore. Your preparation of a series of "lessons" that combine kinesthetic activities with more passive modes of learning (listening, watching, reading) are often not only a relief to your child, but may also trigger two other extremely valuable responses: gratitude and motivation.

Your young students may thank you for being so invested in their learning, grateful for the enriching way you opened this new field of study to them; they'll say things like, "That museum was cool!" and "Thanks for having a party about the Gold Rush!" and they may be more motivated to explore the topic further—to learn about other aspects of this subject area.

Don't hold back from preparing rich, well-plotted lessons. You can intersperse periods of independence, space to explore without a guide, and freedom to pursue personal interests that don't particularly draw your other children. But at least once each quarter, for a month or so, give your children the gift of a well-conceived unit of study. Take some time to create them, to think them through, to purchase supplies, and put dates on the calendar. Share your plans with your kids and get their ideas. Catalyze their imaginations in advance, the way a menu gets you excited about the coming meal.

You can do it! You can create a feast of learning for your children. You'll feel so much better when you do, when you have thought and planned ahead. Even if not every immersive experience turns out to be as captivating as you had imagined, many of them will be swimming successes! Revel in those.

Make quality learning meals for your children as your gift to their education. In turn, they will find themselves hungry to teach themselves more, even without your lead. This is the balancing act and beauty of homeschool. Embrace it.

Quote of the day

It's taking me some practice to see just how valuable both types of learning are in our homeschool. I'm so glad to read this that helps confirm my instinct.

Rebecca

Sustaining thought

Preparing a rich lesson plan for your kids will likely please them as much as a delectable well-planned meal.

Day 27

Intensity

The key to depth learning is intensity. We hear about passion, immersion, delight-directed learning, deep-dives, talent, intelligences, curiosity, and other vocabulary around self-education that all attempt to create an image of focused attention and sustained interest in any number of subject and skill areas.

While each of these terms and phrases has a place in the self-education conversation, the key factor that creates the retention of what is studied or explored is intensity. The most talented, sharpest math-whiz kid will not go beyond what is easily attained through natural aptitude without it! A physically gifted athlete cannot progress to the first string varsity or select teams without it.

Intensity creates clarity of focus, the drive to work hard and struggle through the challenging parts, and serves to magnify the importance of the material or skills so that the child is motivated to master them. Intensity in learning is what is missing in most traditional school settings. Kids are introduced to subject matter in the least catalyzing ways, and then are asked to master it without any "hook," for no intrinsic reason, without obvious benefit to them. They learn to passively complete homework or take notes for the sake of passing tests, rather than the deep dive into the material because they must know!

Intensity in learning, then, is the "compelled to know" ingredient to an education. When I was in high school, I became obsessed with theater (all sides—acting, stage managing, lights, set design, public relations, and directing). By the time I was a senior in high school, all of my classes were in the theater and I used time outside of class to read plays, to diagram sets, and to stage blocking as an enjoyable exercise for enjoyment and self-instruction.

You know intensity when you meet it. These kids are driven. Sometimes we demean the chosen passions (video gaming, shooting free throws, studying fashion and make up). Still, you can tell what your child cares about by the level of intensity that shows up with it.

Sometimes intensity looks like a child walking through the house with a full-length original novella and red pen in hand, editing it at all hours of the day.

Sometimes intensity looks like a boy cradling his lacrosse stick wherever he goes: in the car, at the store, sleeping with it by his bed.

Sometimes intensity is marathon DVD viewing of the same LOTR trilogy over and over again, while reading the books and visiting fan sites online.

There's persistence and insistence in intensity. The child keeps at the object of interest without being nagged. The child cares about it without being convinced. The child acquires the vocabulary of that world, without workbooks or lectures.

Intensity in children is not always attractive, however. It can look like throwing stuff, and shouting at the computer screen. It sometimes manifests as taking a swing at a sister or crumpling up the paper so carefully written and stuffing it into the wastebasket.

Angry comments come from intense children.

"I hate it. You can't like it. It's ugly."

"I'll never be good at _____."

"Leave me alone. I'm trying to figure it out!"

"I don't need your help. Quit telling me how to do it."

"This book is stupid!"

"I was just getting to the good part. I can't stop now!"

"I'm not tired (hungry, dirty, angry). I have to finish."

Euphoric comments come from intense children.

"I'm the best speller in the world!"

"I figured it out without your help!"

"I'm going to read every JRR Tolkien book in order and learn Elvish."

Make you feel stupid comments come from intense children.

"You're wrong!"

"Actually, that's not true. The truth is...."

"You don't know anything. (Expert person) says _____."

Intensity shows engagement, even if the expression of intensity from an immature person comes across harshly or brashly. Being cocky is the privilege of expertise and while adults learn how to be cocky without offending everyone in the room (at least, some of them do), your kids may not yet have been "socialized" to discover that they need to reign in their "lording it over others" disposition.

The only thing you need to do around intensity is to admire it. It's intrinsic to the person. You can't "drum it up" for your child. An intense disposition is not what I'm talking about, either. A child doesn't have to be loud or bug-eyed to be intense about an interest. Rather, intensity is measured through the raw commitment of your child to that one particular area that lasts longer than a moment in time.

When you see it, please support it. Intensity around a video game could well lead to intensity in other areas. I watched one of my kids spend an enormous amount of time on an Elijah Woods fan site that led her to discover the wide range of lives other girls her age lead. She is now a social worker. Another child loved the Internet so much that when he discovered Google could be rendered in other languages, he switched his Google page to Klingon and that led to a fascination with linguistics (which he studied for two years in college).

I read a book about a homeschooled child who became a conductor of a symphony. His passion in life began with blocks, not piano. He became obsessed with building them, arranging them, and moving them into new configurations. When he finally studied piano, this deeply held passion for arranging parts, led to his fascination with conducting music. Who could have known that blocks would lead to music in that way?

 Brave Writer

You can't know how the intensity in your child will morph into a long-term interest that has value that you understand and appreciate. All you can do is admire it! Enjoy it. See if you can look behind the intensity that worries you to see the possible benefit.

My online gaming son has become quite the chess player. Funny how we all admire his endless fascination with mastering opening moves and watching international contests for chess, but are put off by his endless love of specific online video games. Strange, isn't it? We approve of one intensity and the other we want to call an "addiction." I've had to learn what those games mean to him and am trusting that they will lead to the next thing—that next intensity.

Here's to intensity!

Quote of the day

My girls are showing intensity in loom knitting! They want to teach me. Since getting the looms five days ago they have made two sets of leg-warmers and two hats. They have pinned things on Pinterest and googled you tube videos to figure out how to make these items!

Terri Enfield Tippman

Sustaining thought

Intensity is one measure of passion and commitment to learning. It's a parent's privilege to support it and understand it.

Day 28

Top Ten Myths About Writing

1. Writing is entirely different from speech

Not so. Speech is the source of voice—writing voice comes from being in touch with how the writer generates language and insight. These are first experienced in speech and then modified and expanded for writing. Valuing speech (even jotting some of it down for your fledgling writers) helps kids learn to value their thought lives, which in turn helps them to know what should be on the page/screen. Tell your kids that what is in their heads, what they might say aloud *is* what you want to see on their papers. Once it's there, you can mess with it.

2. Formats help kids know what and how to write.

Nope. Formats act like straightjackets. They tell children too quickly what can't be included. Formats require a well-planned outline and the ability to hold sequence and detail in the mind before writing anything at all. Use formats following a period of freewriting and revising (revising the content to make it pop or feel more complete). Then the sentences can be rearranged to suit a format. But start with freedom and revise to format. Never start with format.

 Brave Writer

3. Write every day.

My revision of this idea is: Interact with writing every day. Some days read it, some days have the kids copy it in their own hand, some days use bits for dictation or word play, some days play a word game, some days revise a draft, some days edit a revised draft. And, of course, on some days, have them write from scratch! It's exhausting to come up with original thought through original language every single day. Don't require that of your kids. Engage language every day and they'll be just fine.

4. Imitate the masters.

Imitation is challenging for fourth graders. And 12-year-olds. And grown-ups! The pressure to "outdo Aesop" is unnecessary. Read the masters. Use their quotable quotes for copywork and dictation. Allow their writing styles to naturally infiltrate your kids' writing. Tell them to avoid deliberately trying to write like their favorites (except for fun, fan fiction, or as a language play tool). You want your children to sound like themselves in their writing, but you don't mind if they pick up a bit of a J.K. Rowling accent or a little E.B. White on the side.

5. Use a thesaurus to enhance the vocabulary in a piece.

Please don't do this for more than a word or two (best to use the thesaurus when you are trying to replace a term that repeats itself). Instead, when you see a word that is weak, consider helping your child to drop that word and write a new sentence. Add detail, include an experience, expand the idea, and create an analogy. Weak writing is not improved by better vocabulary. It is improved by more writing.

6. Adverbs add a layer of sophistication ("ly" words).

The best stylists advise removing every word that ends in "ly." The use of adverbs is seen as "lazy writing." For instance, "Instantly, she jumped from her seat." The jumping is already an expression of "instantaneous action." Delete the adverb, add power: "She jumped from her seat!" In academic writing, "ly" words can be covers for an explanation of the fact. "The study positively shows the effects of the drug." Better to make it clear—are the effects positive or is the study reliable? "The study shows that the effects of the drug are positive when taken with x, y, and z" or "The study showcases the effects of the drug by using hard data, not only anecdotes." To review: weed out adverbs to enhance the power of your child's writing. Ask: "What do you want to say with this adverb?" Then say it!

7. There is no place for "I" in academic writing.

Not so! Ever since the revolution of postmodernity in the academy, the humanities (in particular) allow writers to indicate their "social location" (to explain who they are and how they relate to the topic for writing, if relevant). It is commonly understood today that writers bring bias and personal experience to their research. It's important to be explicit about how those biases and experiences impact the writer's position. The use of "I" is limited to writing about personal experience, not used for "I think" or "I believe" writing.

8. If you paraphrase, you don't have to cite where the idea comes from.

Reverse the sentence. Paraphrasing requires citation just like direct quotes require citation. Always give credit—you can't overdo it.

9. To grow as a writer, start your day by journaling.

Journaling is not necessary for growth in writing. Writing is. Any kind of writing. Facebook, Twitter, texting, papers, stories, and journaling. The only people who should keep a journal are those who wish to. Journaling need not be done in the morning, either (what's happened in the day to write about by 9:00 a.m.?). Journaling before bed is a nicer time to record the day's thoughts. Journaling only about special occasions, or when life is painful is equally valid to the "daily diary." Let journaling be the individual's choice.

10. Do not help your child write.

This is my favorite myth to bust! No child learned to speak in isolation or without scripts given to that child to repeat. Likewise, it is entirely too challenging for children to go from barely reading and handwriting to transcribing their own thoughts all the time. It's perfectly fine for you to jot things down for them, or to dictate their own words back to them as they write, or for the final product to be a mixture of your words and theirs. This is how every other practice in a child's life happens—you help until they can do it alone.

Writing works the same way.

Go forth and support good writing practices!

Quote of the day

"When I was a kid and got stuck writing essays, my mom would say, 'Just tell me what you want to say.' Then she would transcribe it while I talked. Suddenly, I had a rough draft.

Sarah Lenard Lancaster

Sustaining thought

Encourage your kids to express themselves but offer help with transcription until they can write on their own.

 Brave Writer

Day 29

A Solution Will Emerge

What should you do when your educational methods make your child miserable?

Contend for your theories of education—explain/share them with your child, and why you think they will work.

Offer empathy to your dispirited child. Accept and honor the child's experience.

Use creativity to troubleshoot. Somewhere between these two points of view (yours and his or hers) a solution will emerge.

Quote of the day

I would say you gotta get creative. Once my kid's upset there's no more learnin' happening! Once he gets to the "miserable" point, we take a break for awhile. I do research (that's how I found Brave Writer) and start trying new things to see what does work. This is our first year homeschooling so I am starting to learn how he learns. Hopefully we won't be getting to any more miserable points.

Amber Charles

Sustaining thought

Empathy and acceptance are two keys to soothing misery and resolving conflict.

 Brave Writer

Day 30

The Four Principles
of a Healthy Homeschool

1. Provide meaning-rich materials for the essential subjects (Three Rs + history/science).

Not just drill, not just workbooks (though there is a place for both), but materials that help make connections between what is being learned and how it fits into this glorious time and space we inhabit.

2. Follow inspiration whenever and wherever she leads (she is not a lengthy visitor).

If you follow inspiration when it hits ("Hey, let's go bird watching at the Nature Center today—the sun is out!"), you will bring joy and freedom into your homeschool. If you ignore inspired ideas in favor of "the schedule," the surprise and sparkle of learning will fade. Don't worry. No one is inspired every day.

3. Create a predictable, pleasant routine for when inspiration flags (most of your days).

Keep it steady, vary it with context (change the sequence of what you do, add special foods or drinks, fill out pages on the back deck or in front of a fire, go to the library or coffee shop once in a while), follow Charlotte Mason's "short lessons" principle—full attention, commitment to excellence—stop! Even if only after a couple of minutes. Let your days begin the same way each day.

4. Expose your children to a wide variety of experiences, subject matter, life skills, and places.

Get out there! Meet people unlike you, take up sports you don't know how to play, go to plays, learn to build or bake or sculpt or garden, see a ballet or an opera, toy with foreign languages or learn one, visit all kinds of places (worship centers, historical sites, courthouses, basketball arenas, ice skating rinks, music halls, factories, Little Saigon, foreign countries, farms, cities, skyscrapers, battlefields, a dance studio, your state capitol, a college campus...). Create vision for what it means to be an adult—let your children *see* adulthood in action in all the places it happens.

If you do these things for a decade or more, your kids will get a great education!

Quote of the day

Inspiring!

Carrie Fogel Geiger

Sustaining thought

Meaningful materials, inspiration, a pleasant and predictable routine, and a variety of experiences, subject matter, life skills, and places to visit will enrich your homeschool and give your kids a great and memorable education.

Day 31

Getting Stuff Done

The number one way to improve your homeschool experience is to do it.

Do stuff.

Do something every day.

Sometimes your kids will have the best ideas or questions:

>*"Let's catch tadpoles in the creek!"*
>
>*"I want to write a letter to Aunt Anna in Germany!"*
>
>*"Can we watch Frozen while we eat lunch?"*
>
>*"How much money do I need to save to buy an American Girl doll and how can I get it?"*
>
>*"I want to see the moon through a telescope."*
>
>*"I can skip count while I jump rope. Wanna see?"*

Sometimes you'll have the best ideas:

>*"Let's learn measurements by making cupcakes and pies."*
>
>*"It's a gorgeous day—let's take the math books out to a blanket in the backyard."*
>
>*"I heard the zoo has a discount for kids. Want to go today?"*
>
>*"How about building a fort with these blankets while*

I read to you from the history book?"

"Want to play dress up and act out the Boston Tea Party?"

*"Let's call Myra and ask her kids to help us make a
Pony Express with bikes."*

Even without inspiration, if you simply do *one* thing
each day, you will make progress and pacify the guilt gremlins.

Here are the "ones" that help:

Read aloud one chapter.

Do one math page.

Handwrite one sentence.

Paint one picture.

Build one Lego set.

Eat one healthy meal.

Take one neighborhood walk.

Identify one bird at the feeder.

Make one historical reference.

Have one meaningful conversation with one child.

So here's your chance! Get to it.

Brave Writer

Quote of the day

I couldn't bring myself to break out the book work today so we turned everything into friendly competition: a math flash card competition, a race around the neighborhood, the silliest accent during read aloud, fastest speller, quickest to locate continents on a blank map. My oldest kids are seven and eight and are pretty much game for anything, especially when we put the textbooks away and change it up. We may end the night with speed painting: 5-minute Picasso replica with watercolors.

Corina Evans Kernan

Sustaining thought

Follow the muse where she leads and see your homeschool become more like the one that lives in your imagination!

Day 32

Keep Doing What Works

In all your efforts to create momentum, don't undermine it when it happens—when joy, well-being, progress, and peace are visiting your family and home, enjoy them!

If life, learning, and love are setting up shop in your living room, keep going!

Follow my mantra: "Status quo, baby!"

You get points for nothing more than getting up in the morning and doing what you've been doing.

It's easy to be seduced by the fawning of fans over a program you don't use and its rainbow of promises.

Sometimes your need to create chaos so you have something hard to work on will override and undermine the pleasure and peace you've recently achieved. Don't do it! Stay the course.

"Make peace with the peace. That's the sound of your life working" (Elliott).

Don't worry, either. It won't last. Before you know it, another problem will crash your gates so you can sink your teeth into worry once again.

© Julie (Bogart) Sweeney | bravewriter.com   Brave Writer

For now, though, relax. Breathe deeply. Appreciate the happy little humans underfoot. Be glad you don't have to spend more money or learn a new product. Enjoy the workable plan you've massaged into being.

"Status quo, baby."

Sometimes the status quo *is* the radical choice for well being. Embrace it. Love it. Live it.

Keep going.

Quote of the day

Can you record your messages so I can create a Julie playlist? A la "Deep Thoughts With Jack Handy?" Just throwing it out there. You'll be happy to know my seven-year-old wore his Batman undies over his pants to a homeschool event this morning. Nobody batted an eye.

Vanessa Novissimo Wright

Sustaining thought

"Make peace with the peace. That's the sound of your life working." Susan Elliott, *Getting Past Your Past*

Day 33

Make Progress with Your Teens

Here's a list of "one things" your teen can do to turn the day around.

- Read (anything, everything—websites, books, articles, instructions for how to play, song lyrics, discussion boards, comic books).

- Contribute online to a discussion.

- Have a conversation with a sibling.

- Solve a problem (math, plumbing, gaming, the wobbly table, the broken blind, detangling a younger sister's hair, mediate an argument).

- Write one poem.

- Study one lyric.

- Watch one film.

- Plan one outing.

- Make a plan for next week that gets the teen out of the house.

- Go for a run.

- Make one date with a friend for coffee and a movie.

- Explain one historical event and the persons involved.

 Brave Writer

- Discuss one social issue (both sides).

- Identify a theme in one author's work and talk about it.

- Investigate the answer to one question. Report back.

- Play one challenging board game.

- Study foreign language vocabulary for one hour.

- Learn one new scientific principle.

- Find one country on the globe that you've never heard of: identify its language, location, political system, and significance on the world stage.

- Look up the requirements for one college of the teen's choice.

- Look up the requirements for one career field of interest.

- Apply for one job.

- Redecorate the teen bedroom.

- Work at the most challenging subject matter for one hour.

- Learn one new skill—painting walls, quilting, gardening, programming, writing java, cooking or baking.

- Start a business. Sell cookies to neighbors, mow lawns, do light housekeeping, tutor math or reading or writing, restring tennis rackets.

- Prepare for one section of the SAT/ACT.

- Surf, ski, longboard, throw a Frisbee, golf, swim, cartwheel, bounce on a trampoline, toss a baseball, hike.

- Play one game of chess.

- Start a blog or Tumblr.

- Tweet.

- Take one picture and post to Instagram.
- Make one to-do list, then "to do" it.

You may need to post this list so that the teen has something to look at when boredom inevitably sets in.

Good luck!

Quote of the day

Awesome list!

Sarah Thompson

Sustaining thought

Expand your teen's world with one of the day brighteners on the list.

 Brave Writer

Day 34

Match the Cure to the Ailment

Remember when you had a colicky baby and nothing worked to calm her? You rocked her, nursed her again for the 15th time only to have her spit it all up. You held her football style, you took her for a drive in the car, you gave her yet another dose of baby Tylenol. Still she screamed and arched her back, wriggled and twisted in your arms.

Later that day, a friend mentioned the odious possibility of "pinworms." Pinworms! They cause babies and toddlers to squirm and cry. Nothing soothes the little ones, apart from ejecting the tiny thread-like residents from the anus.

Drinking a single dose of chalky medicine does the trick. It's over-the-counter, inexpensive, and painless. Like a miracle, that baby sleeps again—like a baby.

In our attempts to help our kids perform better in our homeschools, sometimes we miss the real source of listlessness, fatigue, apparent boredom, or lack of effort. It's important to broaden the search beyond character flaws and poorly constructed curriculum. No withholding of video games or the tossing of one workbook system for another will cure a child's ennui if the source is hunger—a lack of protein that morning, and a hangover from chocolate sundaes the night before.

Sometimes fatigue (not enough sleep) is the real issue. A nap or earlier bedtime creates an entirely different child the next day.

Perhaps pencil fatigue has overtaken the otherwise kind seven-year-old. You forgot that math required pencil-work, and so did the *Illustrations of Birds* book he happily colored half the morning while you washed laundry and checked email. No wonder he isn't ready to do copywork, right when you are ready to work. His hand is "all-written-out."

Stress from an argument with a parent or sibling can undermine paying attention during read-aloud time.

A cluttered table is a disaster for a neatnick kid who prefers an open, clear space for concentration. But maybe you don't know that or haven't discerned it yet. Perhaps your child can't tell you. Test it. See if it matters.

Extroverts may want companionship and feedback while they work. Isolation makes them cranky. They want you to sit by, or copy your own passage or freewrite with them or watch them do each and every math problem.

Introverts may want space and quiet—the freedom to fail beyond your prying eyes. They may need to know they can do all the problems alone, without you correcting any, for a whole week while they figure out how the system works. Then they can present something to you they're proud of, or at minimum, more comfortable sharing.

 Brave Writer

The resistance you see isn't always about the program or the style of education. It isn't always about the power struggle between a parent and a child. Quite frequently (more often than not), the culprit in the "poor behavior" category is quite unrelated to education or interpersonal dynamics.

Stop what you're doing. Consider the following.

HALT

Hungry?

Angry?

Lonely?

Tired?

Ask yourself if any of these may apply. So many of the issues we face can be solved with a peanut butter or turkey sandwich (even for breakfast!).

Mirroring back to an angry child the source of the anger and offering empathy (not even fixing it) can free up space to learn.

Self-teaching programs can feel like a sentence—a prison of loneliness. Kids like learning with partners and fans. You can't do it all with every child all the time, but if you have been handing off too much lately, you'll know it by your child's cranky resistance to what used to be easy and happily completed.

Finally, we cannot underestimate the power of fatigue to crush the life out of even the strongest of us! Sleep is a cure-all. Get a nap, lie down, put in a DVD and snooze.

Going to bed at a reasonable hour? Well, our family never managed to do that even one night. But we slept in. We took naps. I was not above crashing to the sofa mid-read-aloud to catch 40 winks.

I was not above enforcing a quiet hour after lunch for everyone—headphones to corral the perky, restless toddlers, shared beds with babies, and quiet time in their bedrooms for the older kids.

Match the cure to the ailment. Look beyond teaching strategies and eat something. Quick!

Quote of the day

> *Brilliant! We are regularly doing school in what feels mostly upside-down, inside-out, turned all round and round. Yesterday, my middle one paddled for two hours in the early morning, had a big long nap and lots of food, some reading, a swim in the afternoon and then came home to do his academic stuff in the evening. Completely backwards but it seems to work. I'm starting to think that exercise to school in a 3:1 ratio is good medicine for teen boys.*
>
> *Tricia Peachey*

Sustaining thought

When things go off track, HALT. Match the cure to the ailment by checking the symptoms: Is your child hungry, angry, lonely, or tired?

© Julie (Bogart) Sweeney | bravewriter.com   Brave Writer

Day 35

Mix It Up

Bring energy into your homeschool by mixing up activities. For instance, along with lunch lay out a new set of pastels or markers and brown paper shopping bags and scissors. Cut them into shapes and color them while eating sandwiches or quesadillas (we ate these for lunch every day for years). How about making place mats or hats?

Another idea: plant seeds in containers after doing math pages. Count the seeds you plant, make a note on a card, tape the card to the planter, and then watch to see how many sprouts grow from those seeds. Compare numbers—of seeds, of sprouts.

Instead of reading aloud in the same room everyday, take the book outside with a blanket.

Be unpredictable. Perhaps you show up at breakfast in dress-up clothes and face paints for the era of history you are about to study. No comments—just carry on as though nothing is different. Let your kids giggle and discover on their own the box of play clothes you have in the other room.

For older kids, you might simply set two new CDs on the kitchen table that feature artists they'd like. Then ask them to tell you about the music, the lyrics, and watch some YouTube videos together.

Change the pace and introduce new tools. Surprise and explore what is important to your kids—bring energy to your homeschool.

Quote of the day

> *Education is not the filling of a pail, but the lighting of a fire.*
>
> *William Butler Yeats*

Sustaining thought

Changing pace and playing with new tools adds the element of surprise to your homeschool, and releases new energy for all of you.

 Brave Writer

Day 36

Stand by the Sink

If you wish your child had more independence, wean him or her of your side-by-side presence. You can do it by sitting with the child for, say, the first three math problems, working them together. Then say, "I need to rinse the breakfast dishes. Keep going. I'll be right here. If it helps, say aloud what you are doing as you work the problem and I'll listen. I'll help you, if you need it, from the sink."

Some version of that lets the child know you aren't abandoning him or her, but it also allows a little space for the child to "test" the practice without double-checking your facial expressions or asking you to do the work for him/her.

Once the kitchen sink is a safe, reachable distance for your child, try leaving the room for a few moments (to change a load of laundry, to take the mail out to the box, to water a few house plants, to make a bed in another room). Don't leave to go to a computer screen (you'll lose track of time). Be gone no more than 3-5 minutes. Then check back and see how the child is doing.

Whenever you leave, rub your child's shoulders (or gently, affectionately squeeze them or offer a kiss on a cheek or run your hand across the child's back). When you return, touch your child's arm and look over the child's shoulder. Let the child know you are back and interested in what went on while you were gone. Avoid judging and correcting. Validate the independent effort. Then ask if the child needs help. If not, keep going in and out of the room in the same manner.

Quote of the day

I needed this. Lots of my six kiddos need side-by-side encouragement in order to finish the work assigned.

Heidi Richard Krahn

Sustaining thought

A little space with lots of support will encourage your child's independent efforts.

Brave Writer

Day 37

Word Nuances

Here's a tip for word play. Ask your kids to find the nuance differences between synonyms.

Example—all the words for "smell"

- Fragrance
- Aroma
- Odor
- Scent
- Stench
- Perfume
- Bouquet

How are they used? Can you use "odor" for flowers? Can you use "scent" for a skunk's spray?

Can "aroma" be paired with anything besides food? Why or why not?

What's the difference between a "bouquet" and "perfume"? Which is lovelier, easier to breathe in?

How much worse is a "stench" than an "odor"? Can you think of two different items and why one would be paired with "stench" and another with "odor"?

This is how you build vocabulary far better than using a workbook that makes kids identify definitions or put the words correctly into sentences.

Focus on complexity—nuances, subtlety, relationships, contexts, situations, habits, contradictions in language. These practices help the words "stick" and enrich a child's writing as they "pop through" their own work.

Quote of the day

These nuances are why I love well-written books. Instead of telling, through a dull vocabulary lesson, good writers showed me.

Sarah Lenard Lancaster

Sustaining thought

Helping your kids notice the subtle differences in the meaning of words will enrich their use of language and enhance their self-expression.

Brave Writer

Day 38

You Are the Blueprint

In our eagerness to proudly represent homeschool to the world, we can get distracted by academic achievement as the measure of success. We are told again and again that homeschoolers are smarter than kids educated in traditional school environments. We expect our children to prove that homeschooling works when we get the test scores from the end of the year exams or the SAT/ACT for college.

We might switch from relaxed, eclectic-style homeschool to textbooks or rigorous education models when we hit high school.

Home education is hard work (it takes investment, ongoing self-education about learning and subject matter, stick-to-it-tiveness, and passion). That said, home education is first and foremost the place where your children have the opportunity to catch the family culture and grow in it.

- Families who love sports produce kids who excel as athletes.

- Families who work with their hands produce kids who rip out dry wall and install toilets.

- Families who care about the disadvantaged produce kids who want to help others.

- Families who are hospitable and generous to their own families, as well as their neighbors and beyond, will produce kids who are open to others and who freely share their belongings.

- Families that have a great sense of humor and a penchant for creativity produce silly, artistic kids!

- Families who think a big vocabulary is a sign of being an adult will raise kids who trade "new" words via text to stump each other (yeah, those would be my kids).

Your children may not grow up to root for your sports team (though it's likely they will), they may not choose your religion (though it's likely if you are passionate about your faith, they will have opinions about religion for the rest of their lives), they may not vote how you vote, but if you do vote, they are likely to vote, too, according to their consciences.

Your modeling of what it means to be an adult is the primary way your kids know how to tell themselves they have arrived: "I'm an adult because...."

- If you are a risk-taking, curious person, your kids are likely to be also.

- If you read widely and talk about what you discover in books, your kids will too.

- If you speak a foreign language, your kids will believe it's possible to learn and speak one.

- If you travel and show reverence for other cultures, your kids will be fascinated by people different from themselves. They won't be fearful or judgmental.

- If you play with math like a toy, your kids will think math is approachable and useful. At least this is what families good at math tell me! We had the opposite effect on our kids.

And that's a good point! What is difficult for you? Likely to be challenging to your kids (short of finding them a qualified mentor who can transform how they see that "difficult" subject or character quality).

Don't worry too much. It's easier to focus on what you are naturally passionate about and good at. That's what your kids will see and value anyway. You and your child's other parent (if there is one available) shape who your kids become. Think about the affinities and skills the two of you exude, live, naturally express. Your kids are going to look like you. Start valuing what you're good at, because like it or not, some measure of that legacy will be indelibly stamped on your kids as adults.

Like this:

If you quilt, teach not just your girls, but your boys too! If you woodwork, show both boys and girls how to build a bookcase.

Everyone should know how to cook nutritious, tasty meals for themselves from the recipe book of your family's nightly dinners. Comfort food. Home.

Your dinnertime conversations will tell your kids what you value the most. They will get the meta-lesson: this is what it is to be a grown up.

Do you want your kids to think adulthood means "ripping" the politicians you don't like on an endless loop?

Do you want them to think that education is just something to be "done" rather than a life to be lived well beyond school?

Do you want them to believe that money is the most important part of a career choice?

Do you want them to hand-wring over success and failure, or to enjoy the exploration of life with you at their sides?

How you live as a family will have more to do with who your kids become than any curriculum you purchase.

What's so amazing is that if you keep an openhand, if you don't prophesy doom or overly script what the one "right" future should be, your children will grow up to be even better adults than you and your partner. They have you, these intentional, caring, invested role models sharing their best stuff with them.

This is the best education possible! One that goes well beyond book lists and math skills.

When they get to college or their chosen career field, you will see the fruits of all those conversations and tasks you shared. They will look like you, as surely as their red hair and freckles. But a fresher, vibrant, more optimistic version.

You'll be so proud. The blueprint—turned into the finished (finishing) product of young adult.

 Brave Writer

Quote of the day

Wow, this was beautiful and passionate. Thank you so much for taking the time to care enough about all homeschooling parents to write this. I found it very inspirational.

Susan Stephens-Barimo

Sustaining thought

Home education is first and foremost the place where your children have the opportunity to catch the family culture and grow in it.

Day 39

Memories from a Good Public School

I grew up in Southern California in the 1970s. My junior high school was located in Malibu Canyon—literally in the canyon. It backed up to a creek and stood quite alone on a long stretch of windy road between mountains. My teachers were hip—straight out of college, and half of them home from the first batch of Peace Corps tours of duty. They wore bell-bottoms and showed us slide shows from India, Uruguay, and the Andes Mountains.

In those years education underwent a genuine overhaul. Teachers were free to use their imaginations to create classrooms unlike any my parents had experienced. In short supply were textbooks, quizzes, tests, assessment structures. Sure, math still required a book, for the most part, but every other class burst out of the brick and mortar into the world!

Our entire seventh grade, for instance, held a Renaissance Faire at the end of the school year during a full-fledged school day. It took us months to prepare. Kids worked in candle-making shops and leather curing stands. There were jesters and gymnasts (me), food booths with grog and buns, and more! We had to barter our goods and skills to enjoy the labors/gifts/skills of others. We dressed up, too. Such a memorable experience of the Renaissance era. I've never forgotten it.

© Julie (Bogart) Sweeney | bravewriter.com   Brave Writer

My science teacher took our class to the creek and wilderness behind the school every day for six weeks so we could observe nature, learn to identify everything in a 10-foot square, and then represent what we saw through a drawing, using accurate names for bugs, plants, fish, birds, butterflies and moths, dragonflies, oak trees, nettles (ouch!), and tadpoles.

She also required us to catch and euthanize butterflies for our own butterfly displays. I remember running around the hills with my own handmade net catching them, and then putting them in a jar with nail polish remover, then sticking them with pins, and mounting them on Styrofoam.

My language arts instructor taught us how to write songs from existing tunes, to create original lyrics, and then we performed them. We made collages of our bodies on butcher paper and decorated them with clipped images and words, markers and stickers. We had an open classroom with another teacher and her students, and freely moved between the two each day. As it turned out, I actually learned more from the other teacher than my own. She created a magazine to publish our poetry and short stories.

One social studies instructor taught us how to make Inca pottery. We created the pots, painted them according to the traditional designs, fired them, and then! And then!! We got to smash them with hammers into broken pieces.

The next night, that instructor buried our pots in a field in the back of the school, with sheets of cardboard to represent sedimentary layers, buried between the various eras of pottery. The next day at school, we divided into archaeological dig parties and dug up our pots and dated them according to the layers. I'll never forget being the last person to find our particular dig site. It was so frustrating to see other kids find their pots immediately.

I complained to Ms. Fagan: "Our pots are lost! They're not where you said they'd be."

She responded, "You are having the most authentic experience in the class. This is what it is actually like for archaeologists. They don't know where the pots are buried."

That comment stuck with me. I was having a real experience! Sure enough, we did find the spot where our pottery was buried after several more attempts, and how elated I felt then. We took the broken pieces back to class, reassembled them with special glue, labeled them, and displayed them the way a museum would. What an experience!

In high school, I had a teacher who taught us yoga, one instructor who had spent time in China taught us how to take "cooperative tests" ("Friendship first, competition second" hung as a banner in our classroom), another who introduced us to Beowulf and Grendel (the spoof on Beowulf) and gave us a chance to write our own spoofs or revisions.

My friends and I caught a vision for poetry through this English teacher and one day decided we wanted to make "tea and crumples" (I didn't know the word was "crumpets"!) to celebrate British poetry. We invited our teacher and another English teacher as a treat. (The original teatime!) I wound up making corn muffins with diced apple in them to create our own unique "crumples."

Our high school had a robust theater department. We not only made the sets from scratch, but students also designed and constructed the costumes. In fact, students ran everything: light and soundboards, stage management, props, and make-up too. The director/teacher sat in the audience to watch our shows, leaving us to run everything. To this day, I feel such pride when I remember the theater productions.

I share all this because something got lost in education in the last 30 years. It's become a system of assessment and targeted information goals (rather than multi-faceted exploration and immersion).

Home education offers you the opportunity to be that 1970s teacher who uses creativity and imagination to create an education. It really is better to have a medieval feast with your kids and their friends, for all of you to dress up in clothes you sewed yourselves, to eat traditional foods you prepared in your kitchen, to hold a pretend jousting competition in the living room…than to read about it and write a single paragraph narration.

It is worth taking the time to make a replica of the various styles of teepees and wigwams of Native American tribes in America than to simply look at pictures in a book.

Panning for fool's gold yourself in a makeshift creek is better than watching a movie about panning for gold in 1849.

You can't create these extravagant experiences every day. But if you do a few of them per year, your children will never forget them. I can't tell you what textbooks I read in junior high, but I have never forgotten the teachers who brought learning to life for me, and I've never forgotten the experience of learning that they gave me. I have a fondness for ancient pottery even today because I experienced firsthand the value of design, the dig, and the rescue firsthand. I developed an affinity; I didn't simply master a subject.

Go forth and be creative. Take time. Immerse. Plan. Prepare. Do! Execute and enjoy! Give your children a true, groovy education.

Quote of the day

> *What a wonderful story! Wow. Almost unbelievable. And yet, I have hope that we can find that balance again somehow. At school and at home. Thank you for sharing this.*
>
> *Zane*

Sustaining thought

The adventure of learning is often catalyzed by rich, immersive experiences. If you commit to one or two such experiences a year, you'll see your homeschool flourish.

Day 40

Be a Bushwhacker!

Too much is made of systems and plans. There's not enough hacking through the undergrowth, looking for the hidden gems in our families, homes, and the writing our kids do for us.

We all want a map, or even better, a fully charged GPS that tells us Siri-style where to go. We'd take a human guide, if one could be found—someone who's been there and knows the way.

If there were a single destination for your children (for instance: a type of education that we all agree is the right one, or a type of writing instruction that yields a uniform result), a map would work! We could follow the well-worn paths others have taken and wind up in the right place.

But that's not how it works in the real world of parenting and home education. How do I know? Because every parent who adopts a plan, at some point on the journey, revises it. They change course, or decide to go to a different destination. Sometimes their kids simply won't go where the parent leads—and the family must adapt.

Your child is a thriving jungle of competing impulses and talents—each one seeking sunlight, looking to bloom or grow and expand. A vibrant education (and skill in writing) comes from that rich inner life—or at least, it can come from that rich inner life if that thinking, dreaming, imagining, contemplating person is nourished in such a way that promotes growth.

Our job, as parents, is to weed through all the stuff that gets in the way of sunlight and composting nutrients. We might have to hack through underbrush or lop off a limb of a competing tree to let in the sunlight.

This journey through the jungle of home education looks like experimentation, creativity, attentiveness to the individuality of your child, dialogue, repeated course corrections, leading by example, being willing to chuck what doesn't work (no matter how much money you spent on it, or how persuaded your friends are of its value). It takes courage to blaze the trail in front your child when you aren't even sure where you're going!

But that's okay! You're a bushwhacker. You can beat back the propaganda, you can deny the insistence that your children go where others tell you they should go, and you can pay detailed, patient, loving attention to your children for who they actually are. Ironically, they are your best guides. They *live* in this jungle.

A Brave Writer mom commented on the blog that she sometimes misses the forest for the trees—not seeing the overall value of her work, so focused on the small, individual issues. Good point.

But I'd like to flip this around. Sometimes we are so fixated on a vision of what the woods "should" look like, we miss the

© Julie (Bogart) Sweeney | bravewriter.com   Brave Writer

blossoming plant in front of us—our unique child who needs us to tailor-make a plan that capitalizes on his strengths, his curiosities, and his slowly growing cognitive skills.

I'm impressed by you bushwhacking parents. You see this huge mess in front of you—the delightful fruits of your hard work, laced with overgrowth, twisted roots, and strangling vines. Yet, you keep at it, trying new tactics, testing new resources, blazing your own trail to hew out the gorgeous person who is your child, who will be educated (is happening, will happen), and who will find her way in the world.

After all, we don't home educate to reproduce the cookie cutter outcomes of school. We chose this path because it gave us the chance to do this brave thing: fashioning an education to an individual—a fascinating, interesting, quirky, wonderful, bright child—your child.

Go forth, my Bushwhackers and bring sunlight to your part of the jungle!

Quote of the day

You see why I love this woman?

Anna Lord Brandee

Sustaining thought

When you can't see the forest for the trees, it's time to do some bushwhacking.

Day 41

Curiosity

Curiosity may have killed the cat, but it can resurrect your homeschool!

Everybody agrees—parents, children, media, and government—that parents have the power in the parent-child relationship. We parents don't always feel it, so we get a little crabby and pushy about it; but clearly, our children know their parents have more power than they do.

Power is a heady thing. We do stupid stuff every day just because we've got it. We expect little people who've been on the planet a mere three, seven, or fourteen years to:

- make consistently good decisions,
- to always listen to us,
- to be "rational" the way we'd be rational,
- to show interest in what our interests are,
- and to be happy to do what we expect them to do, you know . . .

All. The. Time.

One mom I spoke to on the phone, for instance, told me she had four strong-willed children.

© Julie (Bogart) Sweeney | bravewriter.com   Brave Writer

I paused. "Is it possible your four children have a strong-willed mother?"

After all—how can all four be strong-willed? It seemed more likely that this was a case where mom was frustrated that her superior way of living was not fully embraced by her kids, you know, All. The. Time.

I remember another mother saying to me: "I don't get it. If my kids would just do what I said, everyone would be happier. Life would be so easy if my six kids would just go with my program."

Of course, right away, you can see the problem.

Life would be easier for these moms, but clearly the kids don't feel that way. That's why they aren't following the program!

How do you fix this clash of emotions in a 24/7 home… school?

Curiosity!

That's right.

Being curious. About your kids.

You're the big person with the power.

You've spent years in school,

you're either navigating a marriage,

or you're a single parent who figured out what to do after a relationship, you've had your feelings hurt,

you've failed a test or three,

you've gotten cut from a team,

you've worked a couple of jobs,

you've pretended to eat your vegetables,

you've not made your bed,

you've been late with income taxes,

you've complained about the line at the DMV,

you've been blamed for something you didn't do,

you've been forgiven for something you did do…

You know about life.

Your kids don't yet. They're just starting to accumulate experiences that will teach them.

Most conflicts (I dare assert) could be—at minimum—relieved of the strain, and at maximum—resolved, if the person with the power (Dad, Mom, Grandma, teacher, adult in charge) directed a curious gaze at the offending child before launching into a tirade or asserting on behalf of the youngster, the nefarious meaning of the act, thoughtless word, or behavior.

Let me spell it out a little more clearly.

Curiosity is your deliberate choice to not assert your power.

 Brave Writer

You can be patient for a moment,

you can choose not to fly off the handle,

you can stop wringing your hands...

and instead, draw on the depth of your experience of life—

that things work out,

that you can fix problems,

that time is on your side,

that opinions and feelings change, and aren't irreversible,

that moods swing,

that we're all learning all the time.

Parents must carry and exercise their power gracefully if they want to preserve a loving, mutually satisfying relationship with their kids, which in turn fosters academic growth (amazingly!). How cool is that?

When a conflict arises:

resistance to the math page,

reluctance to write,

punching baby sister,

throwing away a perfectly good sandwich,

spouting beliefs contrary to the family expectations,

"forgetting" to clean the bathroom,

arguing about time limits for media,

the child already knows that the parent has the power to win the argument.

Starting with judgments:

"You're lazy,"

"You know better,"

"You have to learn to spell or read or write,"

"Your sister is not a punching bag…"

leads to longer arguments and unhappiness in the relationship.

Curiosity can defuse an explosive situation. It allows a child to express a point of view before a summary judgment is rendered. Not just the "What happened?" question, shouted with exasperation; but the "I'm curious to know what you were thinking," question expressed with gentle directness.

Curiosity allows problem solving. If you've got a child who every day for a week tells you she hates copywork, it's a good idea to find out what "hate" means rather than assuming she is lazy, resistant, or trying to "get out of" the work.

If you ask a question like, "What's going on inside you when you try to handwrite?" you may discover the exact bit of information you need. Perhaps the chair is too low to the big table and her forearm is leaning too hard against the edge, which hurts. Maybe her baby brother

© Julie (Bogart) Sweeney | bravewriter.com Brave Writer

keeps gurgling and it's hard to concentrate. Or maybe it's something so silly: She wishes she could use a purple pen.

Likewise, if your child is laughing at the disturbing part of a film, rather than shame him for not seeing the cruelty between characters, find out what triggered the hysterics. Could there be some antic happening in the corner of the screen you missed? Or it may be that he doesn't yet grasp the horror of the moment because he lacks life experience and just thought the bombs were cool. You may not need to teach him anything. Just knowing he's not mature enough to get it could be okay.

In homeschool, curiosity is the key ingredient to educational growth. Our kids are not supposed to be repositories for adult information. They are meant to be like plants unfurling their light green limbs toward the sun of illumination. Insight (that fabulous experience of lighting up within when you "get" it) comes when a person connects the dots in their own mind. It does not come secondhand (by lecture, or requirement).

What promotes insight is the opportunity to talk about all the fragments of information with an interested person.

When that person listens and mirrors without judgment, scripting, tricking, manipulating, or controlling the outcome of the conversation, your children have the opportunity to make their own connections. The actual conclusions they draw are less important than the process that helped form those tentative conclusions.

Allow your children room to grow in the sunlight of your curiosity and love!

Quote of the day

Fascination instead of frustration. I first learned this as a horse trainer. Anytime communication is broken, we typically get frustrated, but if we can re-wire our brains to become fascinated, all anger is gone and doors of two-way communication come flying open. It's truly amazing!

Anna Paletti Walker

Sustaining thought

Curiosity, bathed in love, is the sunlight that grows a child's willingness to take learning risks.

Brave Writer

Day 42

Giving Permission to Risk

It's nearly afternoon here in Cinberia (subzero digits today in the 'Nati).

A couple quick thoughts for today.

1. Speech before writing.

Attend to the original speaking voice of your child. Really hear it. Respond to it. Make big facial expressions that show you are paying attention. In fact, pay attention! It's too easy to seem like you're listening when in fact you are rummaging through the pantry in your mind for tonight's dinner ingredients. Listen, respond, engage (ask for "more" - "Tell me more about X," "What else happened?", "I want more details! This sounds _____ —exciting, scary, nerve-wracking, calming, wonderful, crazy, fascinating").

The habit of attending to your child's spoken voice creates the best foundation for writing. As you listen, sometimes you will want to jot down what is being shared. Do it! Write it down and share it later in the day with an interested party (other parent, grandparent, sibling, friend).

2. Writing is exploration, not performance.

Use writing to explore thoughts and ideas, impressions and hunches. Kids need to know that the context for their written thoughts is a safe place to explore those partially formed ideas. It is not a place where they must prefer accuracy to risk. Risk is valued. Accuracy, not so much. Accuracy and technique are "value-added" features that come at the end of the writing process. They must never govern the process or control it. Rather, the experience of writing (particularly that initial burst of language through the hands) must be that risk is exhilarating and valuable.

If exhilaration is not available as a legitimate reaction to writing, the minimum ought to be that risk is permissible. Give permission, take risks, shock your kids and write your own risky, free, un-bound exploration of a word, idea, thought, belief, impression, experience, or conversation. Share it. Model what it may look like to really let loose. You are the permission-giver and catalyst in your homeschool. Break your own rules, if you need to, to free space for written exploration.

Quote of the day

I'm so glad that you repeat, as much as you do, that we should never let accuracy and technique govern the writing process. I think you hit some of these points enough that they actually start to penetrate my brain. Btw, I read The Book Whisper and loved it. I think of you as the Writing Whisperer. Between the two of you, I'll be set, and it couldn't have come at a better time.

Amy Wilson-Pineda

© Julie (Bogart) Sweeney | bravewriter.com   Brave Writer

Sustaining thought

Create a safe space for risk-taking of all kinds, including writing, and watch your kids express themselves more freely.

Day 43

In Defense of the Disillusioned

Sometimes your life doesn't work out how you planned it,

line by line,

promise by promise,

heartbeat by heartbeat.

Sometimes the vision that dances in your head like sugar plums and happily ever afters and smart, successful, contributing citizens called your children, turns into a puzzle you can't solve or a missing piece you can't find under the cushions...

Or that thud thud in your chest...a persistent "something's not right, something's not right" that clicks with your heels and follows you into the grocery store.

Sometimes the ideal shatters through no obvious fault of your own (though you wish it would, so you could fix it, naturally, like you fix everything else)—someone else's implacable will thwarts/harms/crushes yours or finds happiness in someone else's.

Sometimes your body succumbs to germs or cells that won't stop growing and they take over your organs and ruin your chance to do all you had planned for forever and a day.

 Brave Writer

Sometimes the out-of-control cells live in the body of your dearest friend and deepest love, or precious child.

Sometimes, no matter how diligently you protect them and worry on their behalf, your children stumble into tragedy or crime unimagined and never planned.

Sometimes one of your precious kids is violated horribly while you were pinning new kitchen photos to Pinterest and having devotions.

The disillusioned suffer twice and three times.

Not only do they face the excruciating pain of tragedy, at night, and in the middle of the afternoon. They may face blame or accusation from those they love, as though it might have been possible to avoid their predicament.

Pain, loss, divorce, disease, violation—to the not-yet-suffering, these are as contagious as mumps or the common cold. All who are not afflicted look for the cause so they can stay safe and not make the horrible mistakes you've made.

You didn't do it right.

You didn't pray enough, go to therapy, read the right books, get the right doctors, eat the right foods, follow the right advice, use these steps, take this tone, follow this practice, behave in that way, honor this code, believe that set of precepts.

The list goes on endlessly and no protests calm the advice-givers. They want to believe they have identified the one or ten key ingredients that you missed, that they can embrace, to avoid your fate.

They don't try to figure out your failings to be cruel. Know that. It's desperation. To avoid your tragedy. But you can face this disillusionment—this failed bargain with God or life or nature—differently because these awful conditions are real for you. Not theory. Not avoidable. They're here now, waiting for you to deal with them, not with what you "might have done" or "could have done differently."

Disillusionment is the beginning of new chances—a chance to find a new way to live or love, for however long you have.

It's the beginning of asking real questions rather than seeking ironclad answers.

It's your chance to take some risks, to explore some forbidden secret ideals you had overlooked before in your safety.

It's your chance to have an authentic, self-created journey rather than the secondhand one the books and leaders tell you to have.

It's a chance to pay attention to people as they actually are rather than as you wish them to be.

It's often your first real chance to ask yourself: Who am I? And then another better chance to become that person in a whole new way.

I love talking with disillusioned homeschoolers because they are closer to being good at educating their kids than the ones who think they have a "system that works."

If homeschooling has failed you, if your marriage is not working, if your children are reacting against you and you don't know how to bring them near, you are much closer to

© Julie (Bogart) Sweeney | bravewriter.com Brave Writer

having a life built on a foundation of truth and reality than you've ever been.

Hold on. Face life on its terms: the pain, the disillusionment. Don't judge your life. Pay attention to it. Let it tell you what you need to know. And by all means, find others who've walked similar journeys. They will have wisdom to share.

You are not bad, wrong, or a failure. You are not foolish, uncommitted, or selfish.

You are human. Everyone, by the time they get to 50 or 60, will have experienced the humbling realization of being time-bound and planet dwelling among germs and people.

That you would attempt (for example) to be married (till death!), to have children (to home educate!), and to love your life (despite cancer!) is brave and optimistic.

Draw on those resources as you face your disillusionment squarely. Then see what happens. You might be amazed.

Quote of the day

Pretty sure I needed to hear this from my place on the floor right now. Thank you.

Bree Shoup

Sustaining thought

Disillusionment carries an opportunity for transformation. Yield to the process, and keep going.

Day 44

Standards, not Expectations

We've all heard it said that our expectations ruin us.

We expect a "Thank you" and when it doesn't come, we're disappointed.

We expect an anniversary gift, and when it's forgotten, we're devastated.

We expect our child to be reading by age nine, and when she doesn't, we panic.

About that time, someone comes along to remind us that we've set ourselves up for disappointment by expecting—drop the expectation and we can resume life happily.

But do we? Can we?

If you think about your homeschool, you might expect progress in a certain subject (reading, multiplication tables). When the child is slow to catch on, you worry. Is the right move to "drop the expectation" and not worry? When more time goes by without progress, is the solution to keep "lowering" or "eliminating" expectations until you have none?

   Brave Writer

Some of the criticism of unschooling is the idea that the parents have given up measuring progress in order to avoid foisting expectations on their children. Is that a fair charge? Should there be some expectation of progress—some measurable way to know that everyone is on track without the crushing weight of pressure and expectation?

Expectations are rooted in an "outside in" orientation to living—the notion that I can control what's happening outside of me (my husband should buy me gifts, my child should learn to read by age nine, my 16-year-old should thank me for making his sandwich) to make my insides feel better. When my loved ones fail to live up to my expectations, I feel out of control, which leads to anger or its less attractive twin sister: depression.

Instead of expectations, move to "inside out" thinking. Establish how you want to live, and seek to create a life that protects your well-being, apart from how others react to you. You can't control members of your family, but you can control yourself. It's okay to have standards—ways you prefer to live that are good for you.

For instance, when a 16-year-old is careless in his gratitude for your sandwich-making generosity, you get to decide if making the sandwich is a happier experience than receiving thanks for it. If you feel generous, you make the sandwich. If you feel put out, you don't. But making the sandwich doesn't hinge on thanks.

The decision to sandwich-make comes from your standards:

I make sandwiches for my kids when they don't take me for granted, or when I feel generous. Otherwise, I don't.

If a child is not reading by eight and a half, and you find your expectations playing tricks on you (such that you put pressure on your child to meet your need for her to read by age nine), you can be sure you will not help that child read. You'll teach your child to be anxious about reading.

Instead, apply your standards of helpfulness and protecting your connection to your child. You help your child as much as you can, you pay attention to your child's energy and aptitude, you hold space for growth through caring, not worry—and if you can't find the key to unlock the door to reading, you wait a little while more, or you find help.

You do measure progress, not because you want to stop your own anxiety about failure, but because you want to ensure your child's happy growth in education.

You choose to live up to the standards of kindness, support, and valuing the child over the child's ability to read, first and foremost. Then, you find help for the reading issue that does not undermine your standards for your relationship.

When your husband forgets your anniversary, you get to decide if this is just "one of those forgivable moments," or if this behavior is indicative of a partner that is not right for you. After all, you may weigh it all out and gifts for anniversaries suddenly mean less to you than everything else you get in the marriage. Or, you may not. Living in that

 Brave Writer

space where you try to tweak the outside to fix your insides, however, is a painful, exhausting way to live.

You set standards for your life—for how it will be for you. You can't control how other people will be.

It is possible to create a sense of well-being through your choices about how you experience your homeschool and family. And of course, to add confusion to the whole shebang, it's easy to confuse a standard for an expectation and vice versa.

The only way to know which is which is this:

Living up to your own standards feels good in the long run—you might feel like you are being selfish initially, but in the end you will have more energy for everyone.

Expectations wear everyone out, quickly, you included.

Know your standards, then keep them. You deserve a life of love, peace, and shelter; and you can have one. It's up to you.

Quote of the day

Julie, I really like this post!

Sarah

Sustaining thought

Create your own life and allow others to create theirs—family members included!

Day 45

Take a Risk

A Brave Writer mom asked, "How do I fall in love with homeschooling again when life stresses, sibling rivalry, and unmotivated kids make it so hard?"

Sometimes to get what you need or want, you have to take a risk to try something new and foreign that seems like a threat to the old way of living, being, valuing. If you can step back from your guilt at not loving homeschool as much as you used to and think about how you can create a peaceful home that gives you a break and helps your kids to thrive, you will be closer to a solution. It's very difficult to recapture a love for homeschooling when you are in burnout or you are facing challenges that feel bigger than your resources.

You can rekindle it *if* you've got a very supportive partner, you have the energy to rethink how you home educate (bring in a new direction philosophically or in terms of curricula), and you feel you can find a way at the same time to reinvigorate your *own* life with something new and energizing that is *not* homeschool at the same time.

For instance, I tried unschooling after a long season of Charlotte Mason and while I attended grad school. This helped pull us out of ruts. At the same time, one of my kids decided to try high school. She went part-time to the local public school.

Brave Writer

This was a really helpful shift for us (all three) as it took some pressure off of me to teach everyone, it helped me to see learning through a new paradigm (unschooling) but it also helped me appreciate the value of good lesson preparation (ironically) due to grad school. That combination helped us find new ways to learn together that helped me be more enthusiastic about homeschooling again.

That said, if you are in a season where change in homeschool feels like a burden, not like a relief, then consider other options: co-ops, part-time public school, full-time school, tutorials... Take some of the burden of teaching everything off of you. If your kids are asking to go to school, hear them. To me, the biggest tragedy of homeschool is feeling that you must keep your kids home or you are betraying your value system. You value education. Homeschool is only one version of it. Traditional school can be an incredible learning moment for everyone and a new thrill. Don't necessarily rule it out. We loved our involvement (I've had a couple kids go to full-time high school).

And finally, I don't know your personal life situation, but if you are dealing with a painful marriage, chronic long-term illness, or depression, you deserve to take a break from homeschool. That's a good time to allow the local schools to take up the burden for you and it gives your kids some relief from the painful pressure of home during this season.

Quote of the day

This is so important. Thank you for being willing to shine a light into some of the darker areas of home schooling. Making changes to make things better in your family and in yourself is not giving up. It's not failing. Having a happy, functioning mom and a peaceful family is more important than following a particular method of education.

Jennifer Breseman

Sustaining thought

A happy and loving home—not an educational method—is the foundation for learning and growing.

Day 46

Talk, Talk, Talk

. . . and talk some more.

Writing comes from thinking. Thinking is expressed in several ways:

Action (you act on the thought: Toothbrush into mouth to clean teeth)

Speech (you speak the thought: "Hand me my toothbrush.")

Writing (you finger-write a note on the steamy bathroom mirror: "Where did you put my toothbrush, goofball?")

Because writing is the transcription of thoughts into words, we need to recognize all three components and help our kids make the connections. For instance, action often occurs without much word-conscious thought. We go about our business without narrating it to ourselves in words. We might walk to the refrigerator to get a carton of milk, but are thinking about when we get the next turn on the Wii to play Dance Revolution. At least, this is what is happening for our kids. Both require thought, but one is thought in words and the other is thought during activity.

One way you can help your kids grow into writers is to help them narrate their actions and thoughts with spoken words. By stating, "Let's see, I need to brush my teeth before I put on my pajamas and before Jordan hides my toothbrush again," you help your child to use language for thinking.

You model the narrating of life in front of your kids. Literally be the crazy lady or man who talks to yourself: "I need to pick up the dry cleaning before I call the arena to buy the football tickets."

Some kids (particularly math/science kids, or those who are introverted, or speech-delayed) find it most difficult to speak their thoughts. They can do them more easily (punch the offending party, slam a door, open the bottle of 7Up, toss a football, take the dog for a walk, roll around on the floor in frustration).

Your job with your kids is to talk: talk, talk, talk, talk. Name what you see (without judgment) giving the action language.

"I see you rolling around on the floor. You were just playing a game. What happened??

Get the story. Try not to evaluate what you see; allow your child to find words. You can help as he or she works it out. "Are you frustrated? Angry? Worried? Did someone misunderstand you?"

You can't reel these off in a list, but you can ask them gently over time. You can help the child to sort the action into feeling words. Feelings aren't the only "thoughts without words" that kids experience, though (and mothers often think this is the height of child self-awareness, but articulating feelings is only one piece of the thought-

© Julie (Bogart) Sweeney | bravewriter.com Brave Writer

without-language puzzle). Sometimes kids need help puzzling through actions and sequences of those actions in words.

"Okay, you've finished breakfast. Let's go over what will happen today. Catie, what do we do next this morning? What comes after that? When will we eat lunch? How many hours until lunch then? Okay, so how much time do you think we have for reading and copywork? Is there time for you to play Candy Crush now or later in the day?"

That's a dense word-picture of how to engage through words, but these comments can be items in a dialogue of conversation back-and-forth, back-and-forth. Your goal is to lead your child into language for action and thought. So your child, who mostly operates without a clock and lets you initiate all the activities of the day, can now begin to put words to those activities, can be called on to calculate time frames, can sequence the events of the day, can examine how her desires fit into the structure of home education. All in language.

How does this help with writing? Kids need practice sequencing, naming emotion, evaluating priorities, planning in words. These are all skills that go into the production of papers and detailed examination of other processes and sequences.

Your job, as a home educator, is to talk your mouth off! You want to talk, talk, talk, narrating—probing in a gentle, genuinely curious way, lending words and vocabulary to your fledgling thought-generator.

You do so much automatically, as though you've always lived from this ease-of-thought to action and word, you can forget that you need to train your kids in these practices. The more your children explore language for ideas, thoughts, actions, experiences, sequences, priorities, plans, and connections, the more language will be available to them when they write. Count on it.

You'll also have models to draw from: "Remember when you were frustrated? How did you show that to me? How did I know? Exactly: you were yelling at the computer screen. How might you use that action to show General Washington's frustration when he...?"

You might say, "Remember when we figured out how to plan the day so you had time to play your favorite game? We saved the game for last. 'Emphatic order' is kind of like that: you save the best argument for last..."

This is how it works—a dialogue between one's natural life and language, leading to an application of all that narrating to writing.

Brave Writer

Quote of the day

What you have said is so true, Julie. One of my daughters takes forever to do a one paragraph narration— but give her the stage and a topic and she takes off. I handed her a tape recorder for her to do her CM-style exam this week, and she is cracking me up...I expect that eventually she will become skillful enough in the act of writing to express her self in her writing as well as she does in speaking. As long as I don't push her, that is!

Katie

Sustaining thought

Talking with your child is an essential component of your writing program. Count it!

Day 47

Homeschooling During Delicate Situations

The following message is for you if you are facing difficult decisions about your marriage and your kids—all while homeschooling.

I've had emails and messages asking me for advice in these delicate matters (divorce, separation, single-parent homeschooling).

I want to say first that Brave Writer is a writing and language arts curriculum, as well as a philosophy of home education. I am not a therapist nor a lawyer by training, and I don't want to confuse what Brave Writer is about by tackling legal and mental health issues that are beyond the scope of what I offer through our company.

That said, home education is directly impacted by the context of your family—its warmth, the sense of emotional and physical safety present in it, the shared caring of the parenting team, the security of the financial resources, and the intrinsic experience of happiness and well-being of each and every member.

I find it troublesome that we ignore those factors and focus almost exclusively on curriculum choices and homeschool philosophy. If a family and/or marriage is

 Brave Writer

in crisis, no amount of workbook switching will bridge the underlying anxiety that permeates the home. That anxiety/dysfunction must be addressed. Moreover, if you are suffering from chronic rejection in your marriage (in whatever form it takes), it is difficult to be the parent your children need.

I don't want to articulate a theory about when divorce is justified or not. It's an enormously personal decision, rarely made glibly. I've never yet met someone for whom divorce was an easy decision. How could it be? Usually it is the last exit off a long highway, after every avenue (and both partners) have been exhausted—taken as a kind of defeat—a recognition that there are no more options.

The goal in every marriage ought to be: get as much help as you can to have the best marriage that you can for as long as you can. That's true for everyone from year one to year 75.

The usual tools do actually help:

- Therapy for you
- Developing yourself (school, hobbies, exercise, work)
- Reading about how to have healthy relationships

Sometimes just doing these things buys you time—time you can stay married longer than you thought you could, which is often good for kids.

When you come to the point where you know you can't anymore (whatever that means to you), lots of decisions must be made and a clear head (unencumbered by guilty ambivalence) is required.

In most homeschooling circles, a scarlet letter "D" attaches itself to divorce, which leads children and parents who are divorced or separated to feel like they are second-tier homeschoolers—that somehow, the children in a divorced homeschool family are unlikely to achieve the level of success and emotional balance that is available to the other "still-married" version.

It is possible to home educate successfully after a divorce, but it is much more difficult to do so for several reasons:

1. Finances: Likely you are a SAHM, without an income. It is also likely you have not kept up with your field. It is much more difficult to home educate and work at the same time—for you, and for your kids. It can be difficult to find work that fits your homeschool schedule, let alone supports your life.

2. Ex-spouse: Not all exes support home education. Homeschooling might be contested by your ex out of anger, or simply out of disagreement. You may "lose the right" to home educate your kids. It's not a given that you will get to keep homeschooling, even if you want to.

3. Custody: Today, joint custody (50-50) is common. That means the kids are going between two houses every week. Talk about jumbling the continuity of schoolwork. It also means two sets of routines, two ideas about discipline, two levels of stress.

4. Moving: Not every divorced couple can support two complete households. It is common for families to sell their primary homes (where home education has been happening) and for the kids and mom to move into a much smaller space.

 Brave Writer

The move is disruptive, as is the adjustment to a different standard of living. One study says that the change in standard of living is the most difficult part of divorce for children, even more than the parents living under separate roofs.

5. One adult: With two adults at home, you get a break each day (hopefully). It's a challenge to be all things to all kids all day every day. It may feel like relief initially (and may in fact be relief), but it is also an enormous responsibility. The immediate relief that comes from not living under the same roof with your alienated spouse may turn to burnout under the long-term requirements of single parenthood.

Think carefully about how you will mitigate these factors. What are your finances? How dependent are you? Will you be able to continue to home educate? How important is that to you and your children? Will your ex support that choice? Will the ex live close enough to you to provide some relief (weekends off, driving to soccer practice)? Is it possible for you to keep the house? It provides enormous continuity for kids, if you can keep them where they are already living. Is it possible for you to have primary custody?

How emotionally well are you? Are you depressed, checked out, overwhelmed? Can you home educate under these circumstances? What can you do to become a healthier, more stable you?

How are the kids? What emotional toll has the long-term unhealthiness of the family already taken on them? How can you support them in healing and becoming emotionally whole? Just because they seem fine doesn't mean they are. Studies show that five years after divorce, kids often hit a wall (become depressed, act out), even if they have appeared to cope well before that.

For children, even if they agree that divorce is the right option for their family and experience relief once it is over, there isn't a single child in the world who is happy to have a divorced family. No one says, "I'm glad that the best option for my family was divorce." Everyone wishes they had a family where divorce was not necessary.

Not only that: problems within a marriage (where it's clear there are issues—parents fighting, parents not speaking, parents who take cheap shots, parents who neglect each other) are understood as bumps in the road between two people who love each other. The love is bigger than the problems. Divorce says, "The love is not bigger than the problems." Kids are introduced to the idea that one parent (sometimes both!) are not as lovable now. That's a serious idea to introduce to young people who share genes with both parents. We all want to believe that our parents are worth loving, in spite of their flaws.

That is not to say that divorce isn't the right choice, can't be survived, and that good can't come of it. Recovering space for emotional well-being is of enormous value for children. Learning to identify abuse or mistreatment, and seeing that cruelty has consequences is important too. Showing your children that they are strong and can stand up for themselves can be life-changing.

Ensuring that the place your children call home is safe, warm, and generous is an act of love and courage. If it can be done while preserving the marriage, so much the better. If it can't, then consider carefully ways to create as peaceful a transition as possible.

In the end, the most important thing to know is that every person has challenges—married or divorced. Our job is to help our kids learn how to manage the messiness of life, while providing them with strong emotional support as they have their own (different) reactions to our choices than we have.

Homeschooling depends on parents being responsible, emotionally well, stable people who model what it is to have healthy (as healthy as possible) relationships with each other and with their children. It's your job to become that person for them, however that happens according to your lights.

Quote of the day

The decision to divorce is lengthy and lonely, particularly when you are deeply committed to your family.

Brian Harrison

Sustaining thought

Homeschooling depends on providing an emotionally stable, safe space for your children. Get help, if you need it.

Day 48

You Don't Have to Do it All— You Can't

You can't do it all, and you don't have to.

A good enough homeschool is the goal—one where you and your kids are making progress and growing close to each other.

Play to your strengths. Do the things that bring you natural joy: reading aloud, playing with math manipulatives, baking, painting, freewriting, acting out scenes from history or fairy tales, kicking a soccer ball, conducting kitchen chemistry experiments, doing a big project with many steps, taking on one-step projects, easy!

You get to decide. Today, pick something that energizes you and watch your kids catch the virus of enthusiasm. Don't think too far ahead. Stay true to today's energy, vibe, feel. Invest—pay attention.

Do you need to be invested all day, for five unrelenting hours? No. Invest deeply in one thing. When your energy dissipates, move on. Let the good energy spent be enough for today.

The most undermining plan you can make for your day is to try to do everything when you don't have the energy for most of it. Foil yourself.

   Brave Writer

Do one thing you love well today with your kids and then call it quits.

"Leave while they're happy" is our family motto. It's nearly impossible to leave Disneyland or dinner out or a trip to the mall or a party when kids are melting down, exhausted and unhappy. But if you leave while the feeling is positive, the transition to the next thing is much easier.

Try that today with your family. End the morning or day on a strong, positive, successful note and then...stop! No more of any other thing.

Let that be enough today.

And eat something yummy like orange slices with cinnamon sugar. Sunshine in a fruit!

Quote of the day

This is the new standard and should become everyone's goal!

David A. Bloch

Sustaining thought

Leave while everyone—you too—are still happy!

Day 49

You Have Time

More than enough. No matter where you are in the journey, time is on your side.

Your child should be reading? How does rushing help? How does panicking about time enhance the quality of the work you do together? How does adding pressure to the mix create space for your child to grow and learn and discover?

Your child is at the critical age (7, 10, 12, 15, 17! 19 gasp!). You can't let the child slide any more. It's *time* to get serious about X, Y, and Z because it all counts now. So what will you do? Buckle down? Press harder? Generate more tension and resistance? Put the child in school, ground the teen, remove computer privileges? This strategy will yield learning, and will make up for lost time, how? This pressuring and panicking will prepare your child for life after living at home, how?

All you have is time. There's no law in the book that says your child has to be in college at 18, or ready for high school at 14, or reading by 9. These are made up, to suit a big bunch of people passing through an impersonal system.

You are at home.

Take your time. You have oodles of it.

© Julie (Bogart) Sweeney | bravewriter.com Brave Writer

If you are truly concerned about a child's progress, pick one area and focus on it. But focus on it not in a panicky, "We are behind; you are resistant and willful" kind of way. Focus on it like a tangled necklace that requires your reading glasses, full concentration, and patience as you really see the threads, one at a time, and you slowly, gently tease them apart until Voila! The whole chain slips free of itself.

Your child needs your patience, not your urgency. Your child needs your reassurance that you will take whatever time necessary to solve this puzzle. Your child needs you to look into resources and references that train you to be a better parent during this challenging season. Your child needs you to untangle the details of what isn't working, not just the general panic that says, "Oh my word! He is so behind!"

You may also need to examine whether the timeline in your head is even realistic or necessary. It is difficult to let go of our traditions around education. I remember when I realized that Liam needed four years of junior high level work, not three. It was a great decision to step out of "grade level" and simply focus on learning and enjoying that year together.

He is also taking a year and a half off between high school and college, just this year, meaning he'll start college in the fall at age 20. What's wrong with that? Why wouldn't we be okay with that choice? Ironically, this is the kid who learned to read the earliest of any of our kids (age 6). So being "ahead" back then didn't mean he was ready to go to college more quickly or even when most kids go.

We home educators need to stop being so enamored with the educational framework we inherited from traditional school. What is required, is being tuned into your child!

Have you heard the phrase: "Go slow to go fast"?

If you slow your pace to really grasp the details, the meaning, the skill set required for your child—if you practice and master those aspects of the subject area that are essential rather than brushing by them or giving them cursory attention or whizzing through a workbook without total comprehension or mastery—in the end, you will be a whiz at performing using those skills and tools. You'll know what you are doing and you won't be stopped by ambivalence, confusion, hesitation, and uncertainty. You will "go fast" because you "went slow" at the start.

Reorient your clock to human being time, not school time. Help your children to "go slow, to go fast."

If your child is not interested in writing, turn your attention to his or her interests. Capture some of them in writing. Use writing in your child's presence and be interested in what he or she says (what words come out of his or her mouth). Be an advocate for your child's limits— give the tools and resources, carve time from the full schedule to "go slow" with writing. One letter or one word at a time, for a good long while, may be the best way forward. No pressure, just care and consistency.

If you are lying awake at night worried about a child who is showing chronic lack of progress in a specific area of education, you will want to consult an expert for assessment.

     Brave Writer

This is good parenting. Be careful not to push the panic button, though. This is a step you take after having gone slowly. Spend unhurried time getting to know your child's specific struggle rather than rushing to judgment. You might discover the key that unlocks the gate through your own patient work.

For instance, when I paid closer attention to Johannah's struggle with reading I finally saw what was happening for her. She was unable to recognize the alphabet when the fonts varied or changed (it was like trying to read 7-10 alphabets for her, rather than a single one). Once I "caught" what was happening, I tailored our phonics work to mastering the alphabet first, as it showed up in cursive, manuscript, serif and sans serif fonts. Next thing you knew, she read!

She was nearly 9, but that hasn't limited her in a single way as an adult.

Read the manual, understand the instructions, fine-tune your philosophy, test the practice yourself (can you follow the instructions? can you work the problems? how does it feel to do copywork in another language?). Approximate what is happening for your child. Become a student of your students.

Your job isn't to push your children through a body of information by age 18. Your choice, as a home educator, is to take the time required to get to know each of your children intimately so that you might facilitate the best, tailor-made education for each one that you can. You are supposed to take time to do it, and you are not responsible to ensure that it all happens at the same speed as traditional schooling.

Quote of the day

I had this realization with my 17 year old.... He is doing incredibly well (he's officially a junior) and growing and challenging himself but I found myself feeling a bit of panic because he was going to graduate soon and would he be "ready"?... Once I started to relax I found that I really could enjoy watching his life unfold... and unfolding it is. Still don't know exactly where it is going to take him, but I have every confidence that he is figuring it out and best of all he is enjoying the journey.

Stephanie Elms

Sustaining thought

Go slow to go fast.

Day 50

How Amazing You Are

I'm heading to bed now—quite happy at the end of today. I'm moved by this community of Brave Writer parents. I want to share a bit with you so you understand why I get a little maudlin about how amazing I think you are.

I joined the Internet back in the 20th century (I know, *ages* ago, right?). Homeschoolers were early adopters. We were starved for interaction and support. There were a couple of well-trafficked homeschool discussion boards and many e-mail lists. I participated in so many of them, I've lost count.

I owe so much of who I've become to those lists and bulletin boards. Parents (mostly moms) poured their hearts out. I was inspired, guided, fed, and helped repeatedly in those years, and I gladly offered my own ideas and successes for others to adopt or use as well.

However, not all was rosy or peachy in the 1990s and the early 2000s. The Internet was new! We didn't know about protocol or netiquette. The term "troll" hadn't even been coined yet (that would come in about 2004-5). In the name of sharing and caring, some boards became quasi-cults of "purity tests." There were "right" ways and "wrong" ways to home educate, parent, breastfeed, childrear, believe, and do married life.

The discussions sometimes devolved into harsh lectures and judgmental commentary in reaction to an earnest question or a genuine struggle with the ideological set of values proffered by that group or that program. At one point, I literally withdrew from all homeschool discussion boards. If I felt like I had to adopt a certain vocabulary to participate, if I felt like I couldn't share who I really was (the flaws and choices that were inherent to me), then I didn't want to participate any more. I had spent too many hours obsessing about how to answer an attacker or worrying about how to defend a belief. These detracted from my family and my homeschool.

It's been years since I was a regular frequenter of any e-mail list or discussion board so it's possible that things have changed. However, for me, parents in the Brave Writer community that support each other are exactly what I wished I could have found when I was homeschooling. Each ones does an incredible job of being kind, of taking people just where they are, of not creating purity tests to be sure that someone is "truly Brave Writer" (shudder—I never want that!).

There's space here to not know everything yet, to not agree with all the principles, to have your own unique version of family and education that expresses who you are, today, at this juncture. I'm so glad you feel that way too— that it's not just my dream.

I love the overall positive tone from this group that is grounded in the reality of homeschooling (not the fantasy of what it should sound like on a message board).

Brave Writer

This community is remarkable to me! So thank you for fulfilling a dream of mine—a sincere hope. I love getting to know you—all thousands of you/us! Woo-hoo!

I've always thought it would be possible to be kind, supportive, and passionate without sacrificing any of these three, or hurting others in the process. You are doing it! You've done it.

Thank you. Thank you!

Good night.

Quote of the day

Julie I believe your positive and encouraging attitude with homeschooling helps us Brave Writer moms. You're such an encourager.

Jennifer Mauldin Kimbrough

Sustaining thought

You can be kind, supportive, and passionate in your homeschool and in the world because that's who you are.

New To Brave Writer?

The principles you've enjoyed in this volume are the ones I use to help you teach writing!

The best tool to transform your writing life is *The Writer's Jungle. The Writer's Jungle* is the centerpiece to the Brave Writer lifestyle. In it, homeschooling parents find the insight, support and tools that help them become the most effective writing coaches their children will ever have.

The missing ingredient in writing curricula isn't how to structure a paragraph (information that can be readily found on the Internet). You don't need more facts about topic sentences or how to use libraries. Grammar and spelling are not the key components in writing, either, much to the chagrin of some English teachers.

- Are you tired of the blank page blank stare syndrome (hand a child a blank page; get back a blank stare)?
- Are you worried that you aren't a good enough writer to teach writing?
- Is your child bright, curious, and verbal but seems to lose her words when she is asked to write?
- Do you wonder how to expand the ideas in the sentences your child writes without damaging your relationship?
- Has writing become a place where tears flow and fears surface?
- Is your child a prolific writer and you aren't sure how to direct him to the next level?
- Have you tried "just about everything" and feel ready to give up on writing?

If you answered 'yes' to any of these questions, then *The Writer's Jungle* is for you!

Learn more and download free writing lessons at:
http://www.bravewriter.com/download-your-freewriting-lessons

If you aren't quite ready to make the big investment, get your feet wet with an issue of The Arrow (3rd – 6th grades) or The Boomerang (7th – 10th grades)—intended to help you teach the mechanics of writing naturally and painlessly!

Enjoy your journey to Brave Writing!

 Brave Writer